Bernd-Volker Brahms

Badminton Handbook
Training · Tactics · Competition

Meyer & Meyer Sport

Original title: Handbuch Badminton
© 2009 by Meyer & Meyer Verlag
Translation by Heather Ross

Badminton Handbook
Training – Tactics – Competition
Bernd-Volker Brahms
Maidenhead: Meyer & Meyer Sport (UK) Ltd., 2010
ISBN: 978-1-84126-298-7

© 2010 by Meyer & Meyer Verlag, Aachen
Aachen, Adelaide, Auckland, Budapest, Cape Town, Graz, Indianapolis,
Maidenhead, Olten (CH), Singapore, Toronto
Member of the World
Sportpublishers' Association (WSPA)
www.w-s-p-a.org
Printed by: B.O.S.S Druck und Medien GmbH
ISBN: 978-1-84126-298-7
E-Mail: info@m-m-sports.com
www.m-m-sports.com

Contents

1

Fig. 1: Bird's eye view of the Spaniard Carlos Longo

1   The Philosophy of the Game

Fig. 2: In Asia, Badminton tournaments are attended by thousands of spectators, as seen here at the 2007 World Championships in Kuala Lumpur.

Badminton is one of the fastest sports in the world, and a smash by a Chinese player has been measured at 206 miles per hour, faster even than a golf ball. Just as badminton has grown in popularity around the world in the past 20 years, and has now been recognized as an Olympic Sport, the sport itself has also changed a great deal. Sports science and tactical and training innovations as well as industrial research in racket production have revolutionized the sport in recent years. This dynamic sport has long ceased to have anything in common with the birdie in the backyard or the genteel aristocratic sport of yesteryear. Nowadays, only pros who are completely dedicated to the sport can survive at world class level.

Better and better training methods and game analyses have led to extremely high level performances, which the lay observer hardly notices due to the speed of the movements involved. While until the mid-1980s, sweeping strokes and wrist movements were part of the standard repertoire, world-class badminton now features short backswings in order to considerably reduce the opponent's reaction time.

A good example of this is the serve, which nowadays is almost always performed as a backhand in both singles and doubles matches by elite players, with a short backswing. The understanding of the biomechanics of the basic forearm twist revolutionized the thinking about training methods, as it is not the wrist that is fundamental for most strokes, but the twist of the forearm.

Badminton places demands on the whole body, from speed to concentration and conditions to sensitivity, coordination and finesse. The game is very complex, but nevertheless, beginners can make rapid progress in their game after just a few training sessions, which is one reason why badminton is such a popular high school sport.

In simple terms, the aim of the game is to place the shuttle where the opponent can no longer reach it or can only return it with difficulty. The corners of the opponents' court are therefore tactically the most sensible points to aim for, as they are furthest away from the opponent. The following chapters present the different strokes, running techniques and tactical concepts available to the player. The book is especially aimed at beginners and club players who do not have a coach. The optimal execution of strokes exploiting the body's full potential is the basic requirement for playing top

class badminton. It takes years of training to unlearn incorrect movement sequences, and players have a fatal tendency to revert to old patterns under the pressure of competition, hence the need to learn to play badminton systematically and correctly right from the start. The stroke techniques described in the pages that follow are intended for right-handed players and should be adapted for left-handers. When I refer to doubles, I include men's doubles, women's doubles and mixed doubles.

Fig. 3: World Champion Lu Lan from China in action

Fig. 4: German international badminton player Juliane Schenk with equipment

2 Equipment

One of the reasons for the big improvement in the standard of world-class badminton is the improvement in the standard of the equipment. These developments mainly concern the **racket**, the **stringing** and the **shuttlecocks**. But **clothing** and **shoes** have also adapted to the demands of a performance sport, not forgetting special **racket covers** and **sports bags** that have evolved to meet top players' requirements.

2.1 The Racket

While in the 1980s rackets weighed between 100g and 130g, good rackets now **weigh** around 85g. However, rackets can still be strung to a hardness of up to 14kg. The parts of the racket are **grip**, the **stringed area**, the **head** and the **shaft**. From the origins of the sport until the 1970s, rackets were entirely made of **wood**. Rackets were kept in frames when they weren't being used to stop them becoming warped.

Only with the professionalization of the sport did Asian companies start experimenting with **materials** other than wood. To start with, the shaft and frame were made of **light metal**, **steel**, **aluminum**, and later of **carbon-graphite** (manmade fiber made from carbonized bitumen). This helped firstly to reduce the weight, and secondly to increase the stability of the whole racket. Today, materials like fiberglass and synthetic fibers **(boron, graphite, Kevlar® and Magan Beryllium®)** are also used. The materials have a very high resilience and are significantly firmer than steel, but most importantly have **greater elasticity**. Rackets also no longer consist of separate parts, but the head and shaft of the more expensive rackets are of **one-piece construction**.

The above materials make the rackets lighter and more flexible. In particular the **elastic shaft** allows the player to hit the shuttle with more **whipping power**, allowing him to hit the shuttlecock harder and faster, but the flexibility of the racket head is more of an impediment as it **reduces stroke precision**. The rule of thumb is: the harder the frame, the more accurate the strokes.

Expensive rackets are characterized by **low torsion** (torsional rigidity of the shaft). This is measured by to what extent the racket head turns left or right **around the longitudinal axis of the shaft**. If the player hits the shuttle not with the center but with the **edge of the racket**, it can be returned equally as well by a racket with low torsion as a shuttle that is hit with the center of a cheaper racket.

Another property of the racket that influences the play quality is **balance**. There are **head and grip-heavy** as well as **balanced rackets** on the market. Basically, head-heavy rackets offer **greater acceleration** in the smash, while grip-heavy models are better suited to **defensive play**, as they allow for **greater accuracy**. Balanced models are a compromise between the above. You can **test** which category a racket falls into by balancing it on your **index finger** at the point where the shaft joins the head.

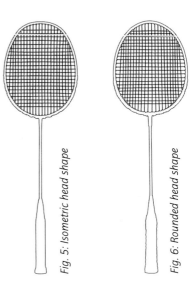

Fig. 5: Isometric head shape

Fig. 6: Rounded head shape

Even the **shape of the racket head** has been experimented with, as the rules only stipulate a **maximum size**, i.e. the whole racket frame should not be longer than 68 cm (26.8 inches) and wider than 23 cm (9 inches). As far as the stringing is concerned, the maximum is 28 cm (11 inches) x 22 cm (8.7 inches). The traditional racket head is **oval in shape** to promote good shuttle acceleration, instead of the **drop shaped** head of the early days of the sport. An **isometric head shape** is also common, in which the head is rounded at the top, thus increasing the optimal hitting area, the so-called **sweet spot**.

Tip 1   Beginners should start off with a more **robust racket** that is often composed of several parts. A good such **beginners' racket** costs around **$ 70-90**. Stable rackets are particularly recommended for novices if they like playing **doubles**. Their lack of technical and tactical understanding often leads to accidental racket clashes.

Tip 2   In training and in particular in **competition**, a player should have at least **two rackets** with him. These rackets should be used **alternately** so that they are "broken in" and the player does not have to waste time getting used to them during a match.

Tip 3   The **grip diameter** can be regulated with **grip tape**. Players with big hands usually have thick grips, which they create by winding two or three grip tapes on top of each other in order to obtain the desired diameter.

Tip 4   New rackets have grips made of **synthetic material** or leather. Accomplished players who tend to have **sweaty palms** wind a non-slip grip tape made of **rubber or terry cloth** around the original tape. The terry cloth tape becomes worn out after a certain time and must be replaced.

Tip 5   **Tournament players** should always have a **replacement grip tape** handy in case it needs to be replaced urgently.

2.2   Stringing

The **type** and **hardness of racket stringing** is an important factor in badminton that **affects shuttlecock flight** and can cause **acceleration**, **control** and **effort** to vary considerably. Strings are an average of **about 0.7-0.85 mm** thick and may be made of **synthetic material** or **gut**.

Elite players used to swear by natural gut strings made of **cow or sheep gut**, but they are now becoming less common as the quality of synthetic strings has improved more and more. Gut strings are characterized by **high elasticity** and allow the player to play with great sensitivity and outstanding shuttle acceleration. However, they are more expensive than comparable synthetic strings and **less durable**, as they can be damaged by external influences like temperature and air humidity.

Synthetic strings may consist of **one strand** (polyester) or **of several fibers** (multifilament nylon strings), and each type is suited to a different type of game, such as sensitive or powerful. The durability also varies according to the manufacturing process. One of the highest-profile companies in this field is the American firm Ashaway, which started producing surgical thread and fishing lines more than 180 years ago in the Boston area. They have been developing badminton and squash strings for about 60 years.

A compromise must be found between acceleration and shuttle control in the **stringing hardness**. A good rule of thumb is: the harder the tension, the greater the control and shuttle security, at the expense of acceleration. **Beginners** and **experienced match players** should choose a hardness of **around 7.5-10 kg** (16.5-22 pounds) in order to obtain good durability. Only **pros** choose hardnesses of **between 11 and 14 kg** (24 and 31 pounds). Their good technique and strength allows them to compensate for these weaknesses. The strings often break when the stringing is this hard if the shuttle is hit at the edge of the racket instead of cleanly in the middle of the racket.

Tip 1: After the game, rackets should be put into a **racket cover** so that the stringing is not damaged by **climatic conditions**.

Tip 2: With regular training once or twice per week, a racket should be restrung **approx. every 6 months**, even if it is not broken, as the **regular tension decreases** over time, thus affecting stroke precision.

Tip 3: If a **training racket** string breaks, the racket can be repaired with a **repair string**. This should not be done more than once, as the broken string has already reduced the regular tension of the stringing anyway.

Tip 4: If a **match racket** string breaks, it is advisable to immediately cut the other strings with **scissors**. This is particularly done by pros with a **high stringing hardness** in order to stop the **racket frame** from **becoming warped**.

Tip 5: Players with 'tennis elbow' can play with a soft, nylon stringing to relieve elbow pain. They should seek expert advice as to the right strings to buy.

2.3   The Shuttlecock

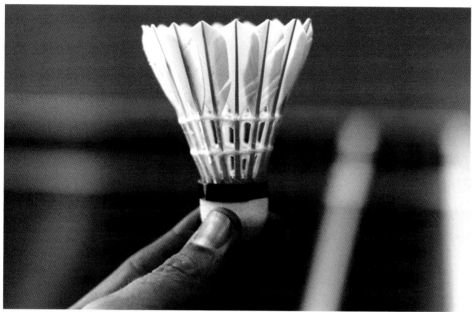

Fig 7: Shuttlecock with 16 goose feathers.

The **size** and **weight** of the shuttle (or shuttlecock; in the US also called Birdie) are specified in the **rulebook** (see chapter 20). There are two different types: **plastic shuttles** or those made of **natural goose and duck feathers**. While the stringing industry has managed to virtually replace natural products with synthetic ones, this is not the case for shuttles. Only natural shuttles are used in elite badminton, which, although more expensive and less durable than plastic ones, have much better flight qualities.

Fig. 8: In the Victor shuttlecock factory in Nanjing in China, the distance between each individual feather is checked by hand.

15

The manufacturing of natural feather shuttles is **extremely labor-intensive**, which is why they are only produced in Asia, although the majority of **cork bases** come from Portugal. The goose feathers are sorted and washed with soap and bleach and dried. Later they are sorted into left and right bending feathers. Only the cutting of the feathers is done by machine. The **16 feathers** are put into the cork base by hand and fixed with glue and thread.

Fig. 9: Follow-through of a shuttle hit

Before the shuttles are packed by the dozen in cardboard tubes, each one is tested with a machine or by hand for its **speed** and **flight path** and classified accordingly. The best shuttles fly in a **deep underhand stroke** from the back boundary line **up to 1-2.5 feet** in front of the opposite base line **(speed test)**.

Depending on the manufacturer, there are different designations/names for the shuttle qualities. The following speed data have become internationally accepted: **76 (slow)**, **77 (medium)** and **78 (fast)**. Most National Badminton Associations have chosen the top shuttles of the three manufacturers Yonex (Aerosena 20), Head (Air Power 70) and Victor (Champion) for the national league and top class tournaments.

Fig 10: During a match, professional players use more than 40 shuttles. Here the Dane Peter Gade changes a shuttle with a service judge.

The relatively high cost of shuttlecocks makes badminton quite an **expensive sport**. A tube of a dozen shuttles costs between $ 10 and $ 20, and **4-6 shuttles** are used in an intensive game. Pros who change the shuttle as a preventive measure after a hard smash can even go through **30-40 shuttles** in one game, as in most cases single **feathers break**, which completely alters the flight quality of the shuttle.

Unlike natural shuttles, synthetic ones last for one or two whole training sessions, or two or three games. Even if the manufacturers continue to try to convince us that their plastic shuttles have similar flight qualities to goose feather ones, experience on the court indicates otherwise. Plastic shuttles **lose speed** in the air more quickly. They may need to be **hit harder** and there is **less accuracy**, particularly during short net play.

Fig. 11: Cross-section of a shuttle

Synthetic shuttles are marketed with three different speeds: **red (fast)**, **blue (medium)** and **green (slow)**. The court temperature also determines which category should be chosen. The warmer the court temperature, the quicker the shuttle should be.

Tip 1: **Over-quick shuttles** are slowed down by either every second or every fourth feather being **slightly bent outward** at the tip. If shuttles are too slow, the feathers should be bent inwards.

Tip 2: Shuttles that have been too **long in storage** tend to become **dry and brittle**. By keeping the shuttles separate and **briefly steaming** them, they can be "refreshed" so that they don't break so quickly and last longer.

Tip 3: Used tournament shuttles should not just be **thrown away**, as they can still be used in training. Even completely "bald" shuttles can be used for **shuttle machine** drills.

Tip 4: Even the **empty shuttle tubes** can be reused by banging two tubes together to **make a noise** during competitions. Fans in Asia have long supported their **favorites** in this way.

2.4   Shoes

Several manufacturers produce special badminton shoes, which feature a **non-slip sole** for indoor courts and a **very flat sole**, so that the player has good contact with the floor at all times and **does not twist his ankle** during the often dynamic movements. Badminton shoes are **reinforced at the toes**, so that they don't wear out too quickly when the feet are dragged – especially during lunges. The soles should also have cushioning as badminton players jump a lot. Good shoes cost between $ 70 and $ 120.

Tip 1: When purchasing shoes, make sure that the **soles** will not **mark the court floor**, which is not allowed in sports centers.

Tip 2: You should buy two pairs of shoes at the same time, so that in matches you always have **"broken in" shoes** available. You should never play a tournament with **new shoes** as you will quickly get **blisters** on your feet.

Tip 3: Always **tie your laces properly** so that your feet sit snugly in your shoes, and to avoid you **twisting your ankle**.

Tip 4: Never play badminton in **jogging or running shoes** as they are designed for running in a straight line and are totally unsuited to **sudden forwards and backwards jumps**. The very high, cushioned soles of jogging shoes will almost certainly lead to a **twisted ankle**.

Tip 5: Players with **skew foot**, **splay foot** or **flat feet** should have a **sports orthotic** in their shoes. Otherwise there is a danger that the sudden movements are not adequately cushioned by the feet and the shock travels directly to the **knees**.

2.5   Clothing

Badminton players should above all wear **comfortable clothing**. Baggy trousers or tight skirts are unsuitable as they restrict **flexibility**. Match players, both men and women, usually wear **polo shirts** and **shorts**. Tightly fitting clothing can also be worn if desired. Shirts should be made of a **breathable fabric** so that the player doesn't feel suffocated after a long rally.

Team players wear a uniform team kit. Your kit should also include a **sweat suit**. Sooner or later, every player will need a **large bag** in which to store all training and match equipment, which has room for shoes, clothing, rackets and shuttles as well as something to eat and drink. Special badminton bags are designed so that that they can also be carried comfortably on the back like a **rucksack**.

Tip 1: In **tournaments**, take as **many shirts** as you have games. A sweaty shirt should be **removed** immediately after the game and be replaced by **a dry one**, otherwise the player may catch a **cold** due to drafts.

Tip 2: After a game or during a long training break, players should always slip on a **sweat suit** so as not to **get cold**, or else they will stiffen up and **the muscles** will be cold when play resumes.

Tip 3: Players with **very sweaty feet** should buy **special socks** that absorb the **moisture** well. It is not advisable to wear two pairs of socks one on top of the other as this can cause **blisters**.

Tip 4: Pro players do not usually tuck their **shirt into their shorts**, as it stops the **umpire** from clearly seeing whether the shuttle is really hit below the **waist**, and they try in this way to get away with hitting the **serve** from a slightly higher position.

Fig. 12: Two-time world champion Xie Xingfang from China cuts a fashionable figure on court with this sleeveless shirt.

Fig. 13: Carola Bott in a trendy outfit.

3

Fig. 14: The correct grip

3 Types of Grip

The **correct racket grip** is the foundation for effective strokes and essential for improving your playing level. This is the only way to achieve the **ideal backswing**, the **ideal power transmission** and to be able to **hit** the shuttle **in the right place**. The so-called **frying pan grip** (Fig. 15), in which the player holds the racket like a pan or a flyswatter, is totally unsuitable. This is a typical beginner's error and can cause so-called **tennis elbow** if not corrected. In the correct position, the racket head is held at **about 90°** to the frying pan grip position.

Beginners should start off using only the **universal grip** (Fig. 14), which allows all strokes to be played safely and effectively. It involves the player holding the racket so that when he holds it out in front of him he can only see the shaft and the frame, not the strings. The hitting surface is then in a sense an **extension of the palm of the hand**. The hand is wrapped around the handle and the **lower edge of the hand** is level with the **end of the racket handle**. Beginners should try very hard to adopt the correct universal grip right from the start, as once any errors become ingrained they are very hard to eliminate later on, and **frustration** is the result when an incorrect grip means that the ground strokes cannot be mastered successfully.

Fig. 15: Not like this! The frying pan grip.

Fig. 16: The short grip

Depending on the game situation, experienced badminton players vary their grip in order to be able to play certain strokes more effectively. In the **short grip** (Fig. 16) the player grips the racket as high up the handle as possible, thus shortening the lever between the hitting surface and the hitting hand and enabling the shuttle to be hit with extra power. This grip is used when the shuttle needs to be **"killed" at the net**, i.e. hit as safely as possible into the opponent's court.

This grip can also be used effectively in the **drive**, because this is also a powerful stroke that does not require a long backswing. The shuttle is often pushed rather than hit. The player's forearm is almost at right-angles to the racket shaft.

Fig. 17: The long grip

Another variation of the universal grip is the **long grip** (Fig. 17) in which the player holds the handle right at the end. This allows for **great acceleration**, as the lever between the hitting hand and the racket head is lengthened. The grip can be used in principle for **all strokes**, but make sure that the hand grips the handle sufficiently to stop it slipping out of the hand. The long grip is least suited to the smash.

In general, the racket is **held loosely** between strokes. It is only **gripped tightly** when a stroke is being played. At the elite level, players use variations of the universal grip to suit the situation and turn the racket **up to 30°** to the left or right. This changes the hitting angle so that the shuttle can deliberately be hit in different directions. This procedure is also **suited to feints**, as the opponent cannot tell the difference between the actual and **anticipated stroke**.

In the universal grip . . .
- the hitting surface forms an extension of the palm of the hand.
- thumb and index finger form a "V".
- the hand is completely wrapped around the handle.
- the lower edge of the hand is level with the end of the handle.

In the short grip . . .
- the hand grips the racket at the top of the handle.
- the player can hit the shuttle harder (particularly for drives and play at the front of the court/net).

In the long grip . . .
- the player grips the racket at the end of the handle.
- in extreme cases the palm of the hand is lower than the handle.
- in forehand shots, the index finger stabilizes the stroke.
- in backhand shots, the thumb increases the pressure of the stroke.

Tip: Hold the racket loosely in the hand and only grip tightly when playing a stroke.

Drill 1: Racket twisting: turn the racket in the hand in order to develop a feel for it.

Drill 2: Feel for the shuttle: hit a shuttle vertically up into the air and then hit it repeatedly with forehand and backhand.

Drill 3: Wall duel: hit a shuttle hard against a wall so that it bounces back and can be hit again.

Drill 4: Grip roulette: deliberate change between universal, short and long grips during a change-clear drill (see Chapter 8).

Drill 5: Shuttle lifting: experienced players can lift the shuttle from the floor using the racket and don't have to bend down to pick it up. Lifting the ball with the racket is a good coordination drill for hand and racket. The tip of the racket is swung underneath the cork base, enabling the shuttle to be lifted onto the hitting surface.

4

Fig. 18: Player in the ready position

4   The Ready Position

The ready position is influenced by which **position on the court** and in which **posture** the player waits for the shuttle hit towards him by his opponent. The ready position is **not a movement sequence**, but a kind of **frozen starting position**, from which the player can think about how to **develop the game**. Within a game, with its quick hitting and running, the player is seldom really in this **imaginary ideal position** for very long. It is rather like a **theoretical snapshot**. This applies mainly to the singles game; tactical ideas for the doubles can be found in the relevant chapter of this book.

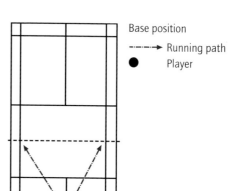

Base position
╌╌╌► Running path
● Player

The receiving player should stand in the **center of the court**, which is situated about **1 yard behind the center line**. From this central position it is **equally quick** for him to run to the left or to the right, or to the net for short shots or to the back boundary line for long shots. This ability to **reach the furthest four corners** of the court equally quickly is the fundamental reason and **tactical concept** for the choice of the central position. Chapter 14, "Running Technique," contains descriptions of different running paths.

Fig. 19: Juliane Schenk awaits a shuttle in the ready position.

In the ready position, the player stands **facing the net**, his feet are approximately **shoulder-width apart**. His **knees are slightly bent** and his **upper body leans forward slightly**. The whole body is tensed, and the **body weight is over the balls of the feet**. In order to be able to return the ball as quickly as possible, the **racket is raised** in front of the body. The player watches his opponent and tries to **anticipate the flight path** of the shuttle as quickly as possible in order to react appropriately.

The player only has a **fraction of a second** in which to decide **where to run** and **which stroke to play**. Every game situation demands a **different solution** and many sequences are selected **intuitively** and **not consciously**. It is therefore important to deliberately rehearse **certain game situations** in practice, in order to be able to apply them in matches. The comments on the ready position should help to build up a basic framework for the tactical variants of the game – it really is the optimal starting position. Depending on the **game situation**, this must of course be **varied by the player**.

In the ready position . . .

- the player stands about one step behind the center line, i.e. slightly behind the front service line (in the center of the court).
- the shuttle receiving player bends his knees slightly.
- the racket head points up and is held in front of the body.
- the player watches his opponent.
- the player stands on both feet with his weight over the balls of his feet and his heels slightly raised off the floor.
- the feet are placed approximately shoulder-width apart.
- the player should bounce slightly thereby creating a tension in the whole body.

Fig. 20: Marc Zwiebler has left the ready position and moved to the back of the court.

Fig. 21: Also in doubles the players are waiting for the shuttle in ready position. Here Danish world class players Lars Paaske and Jonas Rasmussen.

Drill 1: Game without a shuttle: In shadow badminton, all the corners of the court are covered, and the player returns to the ready position after each pretend stroke. In this way the movement sequences are practiced without the stress of having to hit the shuttle.

Drill 2: Corner running: There is a box in each of the four corners of the court with a shuttle on top of it. The player has a shuttle in his hand and runs from the ready position into all four corners and swaps the shuttles over. After each run into a corner he returns to the base position and stops briefly and bounces in the ready position.

Drill 3: Defensive battle: The player plays a high serve and then waits in the ready position for a smash from his opponent. The opponent should vary the smash and place it to the left and right along the back boundary line. The player always plays a high return and concentrates on returning to the optimal ready position each time.

Drill 4: Police game: The coach points a racket at the four corners of the court in no particular order. The player runs into the corner indicated and plays a jump smash while running backwards, and a lunge while running forward. After each stroke, the player runs back to the base position and waits to see where the coach will point his racket again.

5

Fig. 22: Juliane Schenk performs a sideways lunge

5   The Hitting Areas

The hitting areas in which the player can reach the shuttle most easily can be roughly divided into the **forehand** and **backhand**. This division is determined by the location of the hitting hand when it hits the shuttle. About 75 % of a player's range is in the forehand area and about 50 % is in the backhand area. There is an overlap for about 25 % of the range. The overlapping areas are situated underneath the body (underhand area) and **round the head**.

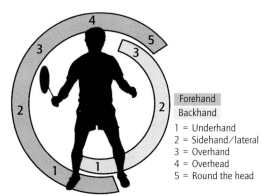

Forehand
Backhand
1 = Underhand
2 = Sidehand/lateral
3 = Overhand
4 = Overhead
5 = Round the head

Fig. 23: The hitting areas

In these **overlapping areas**, the player must decide whether to play a **forehand or backhand**. In the round the head section, the forehand is recommended as the shuttle can then be hit harder and there is no danger (as in the case of the backhand) of the player **turning his back to the net** thereby **taking his eyes off his opponent**. However, in the overlapping area between the player's legs and in front of the body, it is advisable to play a backhand, as this guarantees **better control of the shuttle**. It is difficult to play a forehand smoothly in this area.

As well as the distinction between forehand and backhand, badminton players also distinguish (depending on the position of the hitting hand during the stroke) between **sidehand/lateral**, **underhand**, **overhand** and **overhead**, which refer to shuttles hit at the side of the body, at knee/foot level, shoulder level or over the head respectively. Players should learn the terms for the hitting areas in order to understand the coach's instructions. All areas can be practiced in training.

In the forehand . . .
- the shuttle is hit with the front of the racket, it is almost an extension of the palm of the hand.
- the largest hitting area is to the right of the body, but it can also be played in front of the body or to the left of it.
- the player is basically able to hit the shuttle harder than with a backhand.
- the player usually stands facing the net.
- the player has eye contact with his opponent at all times and can play serves, clears, smashes, drops and net strokes.

In the backhand . . .

- the shuttle is hit with the back of the racket, like the extension of the back of the hand.

- the largest playing area is to the left of the body, but in defensive play can also be in front or even to the right of the body.

- the player turns backwards momentarily.

- the player briefly loses sight of his opponent.

- it is usually not possible to hit the shuttle as hard as a forehand.

- serves, clears, smashes and drops can be played.

Tip: The forehand should be preferred over the backhand where possible; a forehand is always better than a less powerful backhand.

Fig. 24: The sidehand stroke

The sidehand . . .

- The shuttlecock is hit above hip-height and below shoulder-height;
- Can be either a forehand or backhand stroke and
- Can be played as a drop, clear, net shot and drive/swip.

The underhand . . .

- The shuttlecock is hit below hip-height;
- Can be either a forehand or backhand stroke and
- Can be played as a serve, net shot, clear and drop.

The overhand . . .

- The shuttlecock is hit above shoulder-height;
- Can be either a forehand or backhand stroke;
- Can be played as a smash, drop and clear and
- The round the head stroke is a peculiarity in that it is a forehand stroke played from the backhand corner.

Drill 1: Sidehand rally: One player hits the shuttlecock flat over the net in the sidehand area, hitting it directly to the passer's backhand corner. This continues for 5 minutes. The shuttlecock is then hit flat cross-court so that both player and passer play sidehands with the forehand. Finally, the player plays variably to the passer's forehand and backhand sides. To increase the level of difficulty, both players can hit the sidehand flat and variably to the other's forehand or backhand.

Drill 2: Escaping from the back corner: the coach hits the shuttlecock into the right rear corner. The player alternates between playing a dropshot with the backhand and forehand (round the head). This drill allows the player to discover how best to extricate himself from this situation.

6

Fig. 25: Shuttlecock

6   Types of Stroke

After serving, the player basically has the choice between **five different strokes** (see diagram), which are explained in detail in the following chapters.

The possibilities are . . .

- Clear → as defensive clear (1)
  and as attacking clear (2)

- Drive/flick (3)

- Smash (4)

- Drop (5)

- Net play (6)

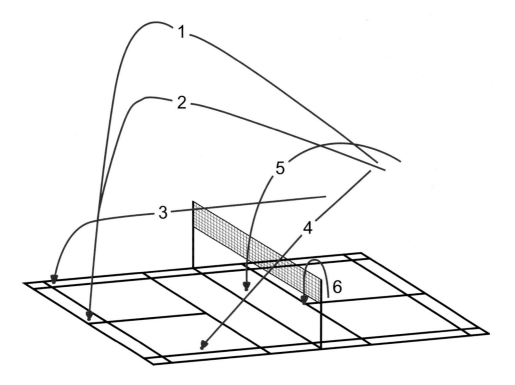

Fig. 26: Types of stroke

7   The Serve

There are roughly **two types of badminton serve**: the **high serve** and the **short serve**. Both can be played as either **forehands** or **backhands**. According to the rules of the game, the serve must be played underarm and never overarm like a tennis serve, and the shuttlecock must be hit below hip-height. These requirements, which are monitored by the umpire, **restrict the type of stroke** that can be played. Because the serve must be

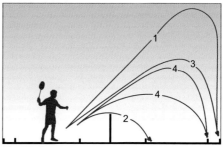

Fig. 28: Serve

played underarm, the opponent can usually **respond with an attacking shot**.

The aim of the serve should therefore be to avoid immediately being put on the **defensive**, and it is important to vary the serves so that the opponent **cannot anticipate** them. Good shuttlecock **handling skills** and **finesse** are required to serve well. As this is the only shot that is not influenced by the opponent, it is controllable and should be practiced until it is ingrained. A **low service error** percentage is a **basic prerequisite** for winning a match.

In **elite badminton**, the backhand serve predominates in both single and doubles, as the opponent has a **shorter reaction** time due to the **shorter backswing** involved. Serves with a longer backswing are also used occasionally. The leisure and club player could do no worse than follow the example of the pros.

Women's singles players are an **exception**; they usually try to avoid playing backhands. They prefer the forehand because of the **greater power required** to hit long backhand strokes.

When serving, the player usually stands at the front of the court in front of the **t-junction**. There is a difference between singles and doubles though. Doubles players stand right on the edge of the front service line, directly on the t-junction. This ensures that if the opponent plays a **short return** they are able to **kill it at the net**, all that is required is a **slight forward lunge**. However, if the opponent plays a long return, the doubles partner covers the back of the court and is therefore on the case. In the singles game, the serving player does not go right back to the "T", as he must be able to deal with both a short and a long return by his opponent. He therefore stands slightly behind the service line.

The server must realize that in badminton he has the advantage and this advantage must be exploited by **varying the shot**. The server has the **active role**, and the opponent can only react. The ideal serve is one that puts the opponent on the defensive. This is the case when the opponent can only reach the shuttlecock in such a way that he must react with a **defensive shot** (an underarm shot or a defensive clear). This is particularly so in the case of a short serve, however, this must be played accurately and low over the net. If the serve is too high, it can be "killed" by the opponent.

The server should **observe** how the opponent positions himself to receive the serve. If he stands wide in the middle of the court, the most effective ball is always the short serve, as the opponent can only reach the shuttlecock with a lunge and must play an underarm shot. However, if the opponent stands well to the front of the court at the net, and holds the racket above the top of the net waiting to "kill" the shuttlecock, then a long serve would always be the best solution. The **flick serve** (Fig. 28, # 4) is the best form of **attack** in this situation.

The flick is hit sharply and flatly into the opponent's half of the court, and is a kind of feint. Bear in mind that the flight path of the shuttlecock is within the opponent's reach, making this a **risky shot**. Experienced players recognize after two or three times when their opponent is planning to play a flick and react like lightning to smash the shuttlecock, almost certainly killing it. For this reason, the flick should only be used as an alternative to the short serve to make it more difficult for the opponent to guess which serve is coming next.

Fig. 29: European women's champion Xu Huaiwen playing a high, long serve.

In the high, long serve . . .

- the shuttlecock should be hit approximately up to the back boundary line (Fig. 28, #3).
- the height of the court should be exploited so that the shuttlecock can drop steeply (Fig. 28, #1).
- the shuttlecock is held by the thumb and index finger of the left hand.
- the shuttlecock is allowed to fall slightly to the right of the body.
- the racket is brought right back during the backswing.
- the hitting arm is accelerated through close to the lower leg.
- the player's weight is initially over his right foot, he then bends forward during the backswing and his weight is over his left foot at the end when hitting the shuttlecock.
- the left foot is parallel to the center line while the right foot is placed at an angle of up to 90°.
- during the movement, the hips shift forward and to the right.
- after the shot, the racket follows through toward the left ear and the elbow is at head height.
- the shuttlecock is hit with a whipping stroke at approximately thigh-height to the right side of the body.
- just before the direct shot, another acceleration takes place from the wrist.
- just before the shuttlecock is hit, the upper and lower arm turn out.

In the short serve . . .

- the shuttlecock should end up just behind the opponent's service line (Fig. 28, #2).
- the backswing can be identical to that for the high, long serve.
- a shortened backswing can be chosen in which the racket is placed to the right beside the body and the shuttlecock is hit after a brief acceleration.
- the wrist hardly moves, thereby reducing the momentum of the movement.
- the shuttlecock is hit to the front and right of the hip.

In the backhand serve . . .

- the bodyweight is on the left foot, and the toes of the left foot are almost touching the service line.
- the upper body bends forward slightly during the backswing.
- the racket stays in front of the body.
- the shuttlecock is usually held by the feathers and dropped by the left hand.

- an extremely short backswing is performed from the elbow.
- the shuttlecock is hit just below hip-height (this is stated in the rule book).
- the elbow of the hitting hand is placed to the right in front of the body.
- the racket points downwards.
- the shuttlecock can be hit with a lightning quick movement at the last moment – instead of just behind the net – with a flick into the back of the court.

Fig. 30: The backhand serve

The Flick Serve . . .

- can be played either as a forehand or a backhand.
- the backswing is relatively slow, so that the opponent will expect a short ball.
- at the last moment before the shot, there is a sudden acceleration that sends the shuttlecock right to the back of the opponent's half of the court.
- the final momentum comes from the wrist.
- the opponent should be deceived (feint).
- the trajectory should be as flat as possible so that the opponent has no chance of reaching the shuttlecock.
- there is a high risk of error (if the shuttle is hit too high, it will be smashed back).

Serve reception . . .

- the racket is held up high in front of the body.
- the racket head is above net height and particularly in doubles is stretched right forward.
- the strings are parallel to the top of the net.
- the left hand is held up in front of the body.
- the player places the left foot right up to the service line in order to be able to "kill" a high serve with a jump.
- the right foot is placed behind the left foot.

Tip from a pro:

Fig. 31: Nicole Grether

Nicole Grether
Born 1974
Record number of caps for Germany (106)
Olympic participant in 2000 and 2004
European Championships women's doubles runner-up 2006
German women's singles champion in 1997 and 2001

Target Practice: the simplest method is to take a basket of shuttlecocks and practice serving for 20-30 minutes. To make this harder, play opposite a training partner who tries to return the serves. Alternatively, one can mark five spots behind the service line and aim for them when serving. For example, spot 1 is the center line, spot 2 and 3 are in the center area, spot 4 is on the outside and spot 5 is the long service line. The most important thing in serving is not to tense up, to just breathe deeply and relax.

Drill 1: Blind flight: a towel is draped over the net as a screen, so that the player only sees where the shuttlecock is coming from at the last minute.

Drill 2: Lighting quick reaction: the player stands with his back to the net and may only turn around when a signal is given and must react like lightning in order to return the serve.

Drill 3: Hold your nerve: the player serves a short, flat serve alternately to the left and right; the partner tries to "kill" each shot at the net. Accurate serving is therefore a must.

Drill 4: Aim high: two players compete playing high serves, to count, shots have to land between the two rear service lines. Variation: forehand and backhand serves.

Drill 5: Short process: player A plays a short serve, player B plays a short return which player A must then "kill".

Tip: In each hitting drill, at the start of a new rally, stop, think, take one deep breath, look at your partner and only then go ahead and serve. Many beginners tend to hit the shuttlecock to the opponent straight away after picking it up.

Fig. 32: The Estonian Kati Talmoff playing a jump shot from the back boundary line.

8   The Clear (Baseline Shot)

In the clear, the shuttlecock is hit right to the **opponent's back boundary line**, and there are two types, the attacking and the defensive clear. It is the **trajectory** that determines the type of clear. The attacking clear is hit fast and low, while the defensive clear is hit high. An experienced player should be able to hit from his own back boundary line to the opponent's. A prerequisite for an efficient hit is that it should be **hit as high as possible** and in front of the body.

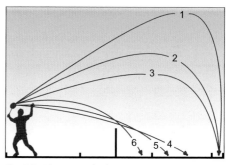

Fig. 33: Clear, smash, drop

The **overhand clear** is the most important shot in badminton, as other basic shots (smash, drop) can be derived from its backswing action, (see Fig. 33 # 1-6). The opponent only realizes at the last minute which shot is going to be played. The clear can also be played both as a **forehand** and a **backhand** from the **front of the court** to the opponent's back boundary line, in which case it is an **underhand shot**. This chapter deals with the forehand clear. The backhand clear is described in Chapter 12 "The Backhand". The movement sequences are can be seen in the photos and description below.

Fig. 34: Clear phase 1

Fig. 35: Clear phase 2

Fig. 36: Clear phase 3

Fig. 37: Clear phase 4

In the **first phase** of the clear from the **back boundary line**, the player watches the shuttlecock and prepares to **hit it as soon and as high as possible** and in front of the body. The player's **bodyweight** is initially over his **left foot**, and the left foot is almost **parallel to the back boundary** line. The **body** on the other hand is **parallel to the sidelines**.

In the **second phase**, the full **bodyweight** shifts to the **slightly bent right foot**, and the right foot moves **parallel to the back boundary line**, while the racket is brought back. The player continues to **watch the shuttlecock** while the **left hand** is also **raised for balance and aim**. The player jumps off his right leg as he hits the shuttlecock.

In the **third phase**, the player takes off and **turns his upper body forwards** as he hits the shuttlecock so that his upper body ends up **parallel to the back boundary line**. The racket is swung through from behind the back, as though the player were pulling the racket out of a rucksack. In this action it is the **elbow that moves forward** first, and only then is the shuttlecock hit at the **highest possible point**.

In the **fourth phase**, the player lands on the floor after the shot, left foot first. This brings the body directly again in the **forward motion** toward the center of the court. In order to avoid overloading the **Achilles tendon**, the toes of the **left foot should point to the side** as they absorb the entire bodyweight on landing.

In the Overhand clear . . .

- the player runs back to the back boundary line.
- the bodyweight is initially on the left foot, while the left hand is raised to help target the shuttlecock.
- before the shot, the bodyweight shifts onto the right, slightly bent leg (block step), where the right foot is parallel to the back boundary line and the body is again parallel to the sideline.
- the racket is raised behind the head.
- the player jumps into the air and the body is arched.
- the hitting arm elbow moves forward and is accelerated with the forearm.
- the player lands on his left foot, while simultaneously pushing his right leg forward.
- the shuttlecock is hit in front of the body at the highest point with a straight arm.
- an attacking clear (Fig. 33 # 2, 3) is played when the trajectory is flat and the shuttlecock is hit very hard (this flight quality is achieved by hitting the shuttlecock far in front of the body).
- a defensive clear (Fig. 33 # 1) is played when the ball has a high, slow trajectory (this is achieved by the racket head pointing backward when hitting the shuttlecock, this often happens unintentionally when the player hits the ball behind his head).

In the Underhand clear . . .

- the player lunges into the right corner of the court.
- the left foot stays where it is so that the player can move back again as fast as possible.
- the movement sequence is very similar to that of the high-long serve.
- power come from the wrist.
- the player can choose either a high (defensive clear) or a low (attacking clear) trajectory.

Tip from a pro:

Fig. 38: Xu Huaiwen

Xu Huaiwen, BC Bischmisheim
Born 1975
Two-time European Women's Singles Champion 2006, 2008
Two-time Olympian in 2004 and 2008
Five-time German Women's Singles Champion 2004-2008

Alternate Clear: Player A plays a low clear (offensive clear) while player B returns with a high clear (defensive). After five minutes the roles are reversed. This helps the players to learn the difference between the two types of clear. When attacking, the shuttlecock must be hit fast and flat over the opponent's head, but when defending, the shuttlecock is hit higher in order to give oneself time to get out of the back corner of the court.

Tip from a pro:

Fig. 39: Björn Joppien

Björn Joppien, FC Langenfeld
Born 1981
Seven-time German Men's Singles Champion 2000-2004 and 2006-2007
Olympian in 2004

Cross or longline: Player A stands in one corner at the back boundary line and plays either a longline clear, cross clear or a longline dropshot. Player B tries to play high returns of all shots back to player A.

Fig. 40: Chinese player Chen Jin playing a clear while jumping

Drill 1: Double trouble: clear with two shuttlecocks in order to practice hitting harder.

Drill 2: Clear with drop pause: player A plays a high serve, player B responds with a clear. A then plays a dropshot and B plays an underhand clear. Then A starts again with a clear, and so on.

Drill 3: Shuttle machine: the coach hits every shuttlecock into the player's back boundary line area, who plays the shuttlecock as a clear into the coach's back boundary line area. The coach lets the shuttle fall and takes a new one to hit to the player.

Drill 4: Breakout: two players hit forehand overhead clears; after each shot, one of the players runs to the center line and taps a box that has been put there.

Drill 5: Clear with scissors jump: the player runs one step back each time he plays a clear and performs a scissors jump. If he makes a mistake with the step sequence he must repeat the movement sequence 3 times without a shuttlecock.

Drill 6: Throwing technique: two players throw a shuttlecock hard to each other; the throwing technique should resemble the stroke action of the racket.

9

*Fig. 41: Olympic Champion Taufik Hidiyat from Indonesia plays
a dropshot from the center of the court.*

9   The Dropshot

The dropshot is a stroke that falls, or drops, **directly behind the net**, hence the name. This shot forces the opponent to come to the net. The dropshot is an **attacking shot**, as it can usually only be returned from a low area. The exception is only if the opponent manages to "kill" the shot when the shuttlecock is at the top of the net.

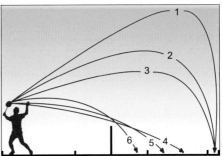

Fig. 42: Clear, smash, drop

There are two types of dropshot, fast (Fig. 42 #5) and slow (Fig. 42 #6). In the case of the **forehand overhead type**, the movement sequence until the shuttlecock is hit resembles that for the clear and smash, although the **speed is abruptly reduced** so that the ball only just about reaches the other side of the net. The drop is **most effective** when played from the back boundary line area but it can also be hit from the center of the court.

In the dropshot . . .

- the ball drops just behind the opponent's side of the net.
- the movement sequence in the overhead dropshot largely resembles that of the clear, although just before the shuttlecock is hit the backswing speed is reduced (the opponent must not know whether one intends to play a smash, a clear or a drop).
- the wrist is firm.
- the follow-through of the hitting arm can be minimal.
- the shuttlecock should cross the net as low as possible so that the opponent is forced to hit it from below (avoid a steep trajectory).
- the shuttlecock should be hit with a straight arm at the highest point in front of the body.
- the left hand is raised for balance and aim.
- the shuttlecock can be cut by the player slightly twisting the forearm just before hitting it, turning the racket away slightly thereby cutting the shuttlecock and not hitting it with full force.
- the shuttlecock should not fly further than the opponent's service line.
- the shuttlecock can be hit with differing speeds. The slower it flies, the nearer it can be hit behind the net. The opponent has more time to react to a slow dropshot.
- the slow dropshot is a defensive stroke and the fast one is an attacking stroke.

A Common Error: Beginners tend not to keep their arm straight for this stroke, but hit with a bent arm, thus bringing the shuttlecock nearer to the body where they think it will be easier to control the shuttlecock.

Drill 1: Alternate drop: Player A plays a high serve and player B reacts with a dropshot. Then player A hits a short return so that player B can play a high return. Now it is player A's turn to play a dropshot, and so on...

Drill 2: Shuttle machine: The coach stands on the player's side of the court and passes a series of shuttlecocks to him in quick succession. The player must return all the shuttlecocks in the form of a dropshot (straight and diagonal).

Drill 3: Drop artist: the player must return every shot as a dropshot, the opponent must use any other shot including the smash and play to any corner of the court. After 5 minutes the players swap roles.

Drill 4: Surprise shot: the opponent hits shuttlecocks to the player all over the court including the back boundary line area, the opponent must return every shot as a dropshot. The opponent may occasionally throw in a short dropshot so that the player cannot get too accustomed to the long high shots.

Drill 5: Alternate stop: the player plays overhand forehand dropshots from the back boundary line, after every other shot he comes forward to the center line and touches a box.

Fig. 43: The drop from the back boundary line must be hit with sensitivity.

Fig. 44: Women's world champion Xie Xingfang plays a smash down the line.

10 The Smash

The smash (in Fig. 45 #4) is the **most powerful stroke** in badminton, and top players reach speeds of **up to 205 mph**. An attacking game with many smashes requires **excellent physical conditioning**. The aim of the shot is mostly to score a direct point. It is composed of a backswing, hit and follow-through. The jump smash is particularly demanding, and by jumping the player increases the angle with which the shuttlecock flies into the opponent's

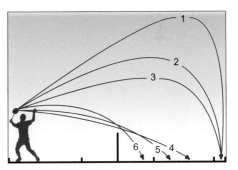

Fig. 45: Clear, smash, drop

court. The stroke sequence can be understood by referring to the photos and descriptions below.

Fig. 46: Smash phase 1

Fig. 47: Smash phase 2

Fig. 48: Smash phase 3

Fig. 49: Smash phase 4

In the **first phase**, the player shifts his bodyweight from the left to the right foot, as for the clear. The player watches the shuttlecock and uses his left hand to aim then draws his racket back to hit the shuttlecock.

In the **second phase**, the weight is on the right foot. The upper body is turned parallel to the sidelines. The right arm is raised in order to hit the shuttlecock.

In the **third phase**, the upper body turns as the shuttlecock is hit so that it ends up parallel to the back boundary line.

In the **fourth phase**, the weight shifts again onto the left leg, with which the player pushes forward off the ground. The player moves straight back to the center of the court.

In the smash . . .

- The movement sequence is broadly similar to that of the clear, but the smash requires more power and speed.

- The shot can be performed overhead or underhand.

- The player lunges backward with a sideways movement, the body moves backward.

- During the lunging phase, the bodyweight lies over the right foot, which stays at the back.

- The right knee is bent and straightened again as the shot is played, alternatively it is played from the plant (step).

- The player jumps up high.

- The right elbow is pulled back, the left hand points up at the shuttlecock for balance and aim.

- The right hip and right shoulder are turned explosively forward during the hitting phase.

- The body is tensed during the jump, like a tensed bow.

- This body tension is finally dissipated with a fast, powerful hitting action.

- The right forearm turns inward, then the wrist is flexed.

- The shuttle is hit at its highest point in front of the body.

- The player lands on the ground with the left foot, with which he can immediately start to move forward.

- As the shuttle is hit, the arm is pulled right down.

- The shuttle should land as near to the front of the opponent's court as possible.

- The shuttle should be hit as high as possible in order to have a good angle to the net.

Tip from a pro:

Fig. 50: Petra Reichel

Petra Reichel, née Overzier, BV Mülheim
Born 1982
World Championships Semi-finalist in Women's Singles 2006
German Champion 2002, 2003

Beyond the line: Player A hits the shuttle up high, player B smashes it down the line (single players down the singles line, doubles players down the doubles line). Then player A returns the shuttle at half-height into the midfield so that player B can chase it and kill it.

Tip from a pro:

Fig. 51: Juliane Schenk

Juliane Schenk, EBT Berlin
Born 1982
Two-time European Championships Semi-finalist in Women's Singles 2006, 2008
Olympian in 2004, 2008
German Champion 2009

Half-Court Smash: This is a game of singles without the front of the court (the court only goes as far as the service line). Play starts with a high serve, and the return should be a half-smash, stick-smash and smash. The stick smash is halfway between a smash and a dropshot, like a half-smash but faster and steeper. The defense should if possible be played down the line (at the right height, it is hard for the opponent to do anything with the shuttle). If the attack is too hard, a straight, short defensive shot is allowed. If the attacker then chases it, depending on where he hits the shuttle, he can push it into the back of the court or lift it.

Fig. 52: The jump smash is the most powerful shot in badminton, here played by the Chinese Xie Zhongbo.

Drill 1: Alternate smash: Player A hits a high shot to player B, who responds with a smash. Player A then tries to play a short defensive shot so that that B can respond with another high shot and then it's A's turn to smash.

Drill 2: Scissor jump smash: After a high serve from his opponent, the player hits a smash with a scissors jump, the opponent responds with a short dropshot which the player returns with another net shot, the opponent can now play a high return so that the player has to run to the back of the court and can play a jump smash.

Drill 3: Shuttle machine: The coach hits shuttles to the player right out wide into the backhand corner, which the player must smash with a round-the-head smash.

Drill 4: Half-court game: Two players play for points on half the court, but points can only be won by smashing, all other shots are just part of the rally.

Drill 5: Forehand smash: The opponent hits the shuttle alternately into the player's left forehand corner and short and straight over the net. The player either hits a longline or crosscourt smash from his forehand corner and must come to the net after every smash in order to reach the opponent's dropshot, which he also returns as a dropshot. The opponent can then return the shuttle deep into the player's forehand corner.

Fig. 53: Ian Maywald (here in the doubles with Marc Zwiebler) plays a smash.

Fig. 54. Doubles specialist Michael Fuchs plays a drive.

Masuda, Keita
Ohtsuka, Tadashi
JPN   1-2   GER
Spitko, Roman

11   The Drive

The drive is an **attacking shot** in which the shuttlecock is hit so fast that the opponent barely has time to react. The drive is played from **near the left and right sideline**s, about halfway between the net and the back of the court. The player **starts this stroke with a lunge** and it can be played

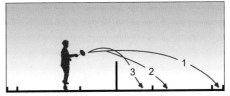

Fig. 55: The drive

as a forehand (on the right of the body) and a backhand (on the left of the body). The shuttle travels quickly and flat over the net.

The drive should ideally be hit **parallel to the sideline**, but it can also be **hit cross-court**, which has the disadvantage that the shuttle must pass through the **center of the court** where the opponent can easily reach it, and if he is in the right position, he can easily hit a **winning return shot**.

The **flick version** of the drive (see Fig. 55, #1) is usually a point winner. The drive is a shot that is **mainly used in doubles**, particularly to return a flat serve. The target area for a sharply hit drive lies in **front of the service line of the opponent** (see Fig. 55, #3), otherwise the shuttle flies into the center of the court (see Fig. 55, #2). The player should come to the net after hitting a drive, as a **high defensive shot** from the opponent can be returned with a smash by his doubles partner.

Fig. 56: The drive

In the forehand drive . . .

- The shuttle is hit at the side of the body and crosses the net with a flat trajectory to the opponent.

- The shuttle is hit near the left or right sideline.

- The target area is the back of the opponent's court.

- It can be played down the line or cross-court.

- The elbow goes toward the shuttle first, the arm is pre-tensed.

- The shot is played from the upper arm, the elbow and the wrist.

- The shuttle is hit at the side of the body at approximately head-height.

- The player lunges with the right leg toward the shuttlecock.

- In a flick drive, what seems to be a short shot is accelerated at the last minute and hit long (feint).

In a backhand drive . . .

- The right hitting arm is horizontal at chest height in front of the body.

- The feet are either parallel next to each other (with the knees slightly bent) or the left leg lunges forward slightly to the left.

- The shot is hit with a powerful twist of the forearm.

- The shot is hit low and either parallel or diagonally over the net.

- The thumb of the hitting hand should press the racket handles to increase the leverage effect of the shot.

Drill 1: Hunt: Players A and B hit the ball to each other quick and with a flat trajectory over the net using both forehands and backhands. After a few shots, both players move back a little after each shot, then start to come back into the net again.

Drill 2: Spoilsports: Players A and B play drives to each other as in drill 1, then players C and D stand right at the net and try to get in the way and "kill" the shuttle.

Drill 3: Shuttle machine: The coach hits shuttles over the net in quick succession to the player, who must return them as longline drives. The coach hits to the player's forehand and backhand sides.

Fig. 57: Vietnamese star Nguyen Tien Min
is starting for a drive.

12

Fig. 58: Juliane Schenk plays a backhand

12   The Backhand

All the basic shots (clear, smash, drop, drive and serve) can be played as backhands, both in defensive play and play at the net. The backhand is always the **second best option** from the back boundary line (as an overhand shot), and the forehand should be played whenever possible (left-of-head shot). The backhand has less precision and power, although the

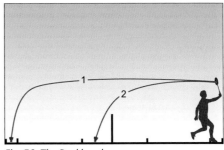

Fig. 59: The Backhand

backhand clear, smash and drop are among the **most technically demanding shots** in badminton. The backhand can be **very effective** in the front of the court as a **defensive shot**, when the player is standing either in the center of the court or lunges to the net. The backhand technique can be understood with the aid of the photos and descriptions below.

Fig. 60: Back boundary line backhand phase 1

Fig. 61: Back boundary line backhand phase 2

Fig. 62: Back boundary line backhand phase 3   *Fig. 63: Back boundary line backhand phase 4*

In the **first phase**, the player runs into the backhand corner, making sure he doesn't take his eye off either the shuttle or his opponent for too long.

In the **second phase**, the player steps into the shot with his bodyweight over his right foot. In extreme cases, the player may lunge in order to reach the shuttle. The foot is almost diagonal to the sidelines and the upper body is parallel to the back boundary line.

In the **third phase**, the player is behind the shuttle, which should be hit as high as possible. The player can press the thumb of the hitting hand onto the racket handle for extra power. The shot can be played as a clear, drop or smash.

In the **fourth phase**, the player jumps off the right leg and goes straight into the center of the court, keeping his eye on his opponent.

In the backhand from the back boundary line . . .

- the player starts from the ready position and takes several steps into the backhand corner.

- the player should keep his eye on both the shuttle and his opponent for as long as possible.

- the player's body turns through at least 90°.

- the last step before the shuttlecock is hit is a lunge with the right leg.

- the right knee is slightly bent when the shuttle is hit.

- the right foot points toward the sidelines.

- the right shoulder points toward the right net post.

- the racket is drawn back from below in preparation to hit the shuttle, the hitting arm elbow moves toward the net.

- as the shot is played, the upper arm provides momentum and the forearm twists.

- the grip position is slightly different to the universal grip and is turned slightly inward (i.e. inside of the hand to the right).

- the shuttle is hit at the highest point near the body (backhand-overhand shot) and in the clear (Fig. 59 #1) is hit to the opponent's back boundary line.

- increase acceleration by placing the thumb behind the handle.

- in the drop (Fig. 59 #2), the hitting arm slows down shortly before the shot is played.

- in the smash, there is a full forearm twist and the shuttle is forced down with full acceleration.

In the defensive backhand from the center of the court . . .

- the player stands about 1 yard behind the center line.

- the player stands with the knees slightly bent and the feet shoulder-width apart.

- the racket is held in front of the body pointing downward.

- the thumb is pressed against the handle for extra acceleration.

- there is a small backswing.

- acceleration is achieved by twisting the forearm.

Fig. 64: Defensive backhand to the left of the body   *Fig. 65: Defensive backhand at the right of the body*

The backhand at the net . . .

- enables the left front part of the court to be covered.

- can be played as a short shot, clear or flick.

- From the ready position, the player takes a step to the left, the right foot stays where it is to enable the player to move backward again as soon as possible.

- Ideally, the shuttle should be hit with an almost straight arm at net-height.

- The axis of the racket head is parallel to the top of the net and hits the shuttle at a slight angle to the net.

Tip from a pro:

Fig. 66: Dieter Domke

Dieter Domke, EBT Berlin
Born 1987
German U21 Men's Singles Champion 2005, 2007

Alternating backhand: the opponent stands at the net in the forehand corner while the player stands in the center of the court. Player A plays a flat shot into the backhand corner to player B, who plays a backhand return to player A, who lures player B out of the backhand corner toward the t-junction with a short shot, which player B returns into player A's forehand corner. They then start again as player A plays a flat shot into player B's backhand corner, and so on. The drill can be made more difficult by asking player A to cover the whole of the front of the court and player B to play a short backhand net shot. Player A must then neutralize this shot with a short shot played toward the center of the court, for player B to return this short shot into player A's forehand corner. A flat shot into player B's backhand corner completes the sequence and it can be repeated as desired.

Tip from a pro:

Fig. 67: Marc Zwiebler

Marc Zwiebler, BC Beuel
Born 1984
German Men's Singles Champion 2005, 2008, 2009
Olympian in 2008
Runner-up Denmark Super Series 2009

Into the corner: The opponent chooses two corners to cover and lets the player run from the forehand corner forward to the net and then cross-court to the backhand corner in no particular order (can be in a particular order to start with). This is performed in all possible variations (opponent both back corners, both front corners, etc.) for about two minutes each, followed by 1 minute rest or change, i.e. a total of about 12 minutes. The opponent should use a variety of high shots, which give the player plenty of time to play a backhand return, and quick, flat shots to the back of the court to place the player under match-typical pressure. For added difficulty, the player can also use a heavier racket (e.g. squash racket) to work on muscle strength.

Drill 1: Alternating backhand dropshot: Two players hit to each other from the backhand corner, so that the other player can hit a dropshot. Player A starts with a high serve, player B plays a dropshot. Player A then responds with a short dropshot so that player B can return this deep into player A's backhand corner.

Drill 2: Backhand dropshot variants: The player plays each shot as a backhand dropshot, hitting both down the line and cross-court. The opponent always returns the shuttle to the player's backhand corner. For increased difficulty, the opponent occasionally surprises the player with a dropshot.

Drill 3: Backhand clear duel: Two players play competitive rallies with backhand clears down the line. The shuttle must land in a pre-determined area at the back of the court, ideally between the two service lines. If one of the player's shots falls short, the partner does not have to return it and he wins a point.

Drill 4: Against the wall: The coach stands in front of a wall and throws or hits shuttlecocks to the player in quick succession. The shuttles should reach the corner left of the player's head so that he can hit the shuttles with a backhand against the wall.

Drill 5: Into the center: The player hits a dropshot down the line, which the opponent returns with a dropshot. The opponent then returns the shuttlecock to the player's backhand corner. The player must always pass through the center of the court as he runs to and from the net. A box can be placed near the center that must be tapped with the racket each time.

Fig. 68: Dieter Domke is playing a backhand

13 Net Play

Net play requires **quick reactions, technical know-how and sensitivity**, as the racket – unlike the shuttle – is not allowed to touch the net. Neither the racket nor the player may cross the line of the net either above or below it. There are **two types of net shot**, those **hit above** and **below the top of the net**. Those hit above the net are **attacking shots** (e.g. "kill," "drop"), and those below are **defensive shots** ("lift," "hairpin," "slice").

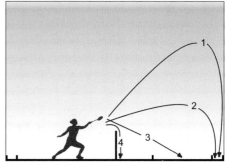

Fig. 70: Net play

The common feature between both types of shots is that they are preceded by a lunge, which brings the player to a **central position** at the net.

Fig. 71: A net shot

A **"kill"** is a **powerful shot** hit **steeply down** into the opponent's court (#3 in Fig. 70). This can be either cross-court or straight. The dropshot is often used for a return of serve, when the player lunges toward the net and almost pushes the shuttlecock **down into the opponent's half of the court**. This shot is not hit as hard as the kill. By **moving the racket slightly to** the left or right of the universal grip, the shuttlecock can be changed accordingly. In the dropshot, the player hits the shuttlecock **just above the top of the net** and lets it drop over to the opponent's court (#4, Fig. 70). The shuttlecock therefore falls just **a few inches behind the net** so that the opponent is forced to play a **defensive return**. In a dropshot, the player almost just holds out the racket without really using any force.

Fig. 72: Seven-time German champion Björn Joppien pushes a shot over the net.

The 'lift' is an **emergency shot** that must often be played though as the player cannot get to the net quickly enough. The **racket head** is **parallel to the ground** and the shuttlecock is lifted with a gentle movement just into the opponent's side of the net or up high right to the back of the court (Fig. 70 #1). In particular when this shot is played cross-court, make sure that a shot is really being played, and the shuttlecock is not being 'carried', which is a fault.

In the 'spin', the shuttle is hit just below net height, the player swings the racket into the shuttle **like a fencer** attacks with his sword. The angle at which the racket and shuttle meet determines how much spin the shuttle has when it crosses the net. Ideally, the shuttle should touch the top of the net and then just drop over into the opponent's side of the court. It is almost impossible to return this shot properly. For the net drop and spin shots, the efficiency of the shot is **increased by slicing** the shuttlecock, i.e. the shuttle just glances off the racket instead of being **hit at a 90° angle**.

Accurate net play is particularly important in doubles. **Slicing** the shuttlecock is a vital prerequisite in top level badminton, as it enables the player to surprise and deceive his opponent. Slicing requires great technical skill as the shuttlecock is hit against its normal flight behavior; it is a **risky shot** with a **high failure rate**. The illustrations and descriptions below give a good understanding of net play.

Net play is particularly **suited to feints**. Players appear to be going to play one type of shot but then play another. Experienced players **disguise shots** by their movements and also by their line of vision, which they change at the very last minute. This requires **excellent technique**, as it is difficult and very risky to change one's movement path at the very last moment. It is easiest when one pretends to hit a short shot, thereby bringing the opponent to the net but then suddenly playing **a deep flick** shot (Fig. 70 #2).

Fig. 73: Net "kill"

Fig. 74: Dropshot at the net

Net play above the net . . .

- the player must get to the net early as the shuttle must be hit just after crossing the net.

- the player lunges forward from the ready position (for the forehand with the right leg and for the backhand with the left leg) → Running Technique, Chapter 14.

- the shuttle is 'killed' by hitting it as hard as possible down over the net (diagonally if possible) into the opponent's side of the court. The shot is performed with the forearm and wrist.

- the shuttle is 'spun' when there is a danger that the player will break the rules by allowing the racket to go over to the other side of the net when hitting normally.

- is 'spun' by holding the racket almost vertical (parallel to the net); with a push to the left or right the shuttle falls just over the net; the racket grip differs from the universal grip in that it is turned slightly to the right or left in the hand.

- the shuttle is 'dropped' when directly at the top of the net the racket is held back at a slight angle so that the shuttle drops just over the net into the opponent's court.

- the shuttle is flicked when played deep toward the back boundary line.

Fig. 75: Petra Reichel playing at the net

Net play below the top of the net . . .

- the player lunges forward from the ready position (usually with the right leg).

- the shuttle is 'lifted' by hitting it gently and sensitively close to the net and curling it so that it falls just the other side of the net; there is therefore no backswing of the racket, instead it is just held back and the racket axis is horizontal to the top of the net.

- the shuttle is 'sliced' by hitting it not with the flat racket surface but at an angle to the flight direction of the shuttle; the steeper this angle is, the more the spinning shuttle is sliced.

- the shuttle is 'spun' when the player spins the bottom of the shuttle at about net height, thus rotating it against the lateral axis.

Tip from a pro:

Fig. 76: Birgit Overzier

Birgit Overzier, BC Beuel
Born 1984
German Women's Doubles Champion in 2008, 2009
Olympian in 2008

Net cord duel: Player A starts with a normal short serve, player B receives the shuttle in front of the service line. The players must keep the shuttle within the front of the net and the service lines and only net cords can win points. The first player to score 5 net cords wins the game. Shots are only considered to be net cords if they can no longer be returned by the opponent.

Tip from a pro:

Fig. 77: Kristof Hopp

Kristof Hopp, BC Bischmisheim
Born 1978
Five-time German Men's Doubles Champion, one-time Mixed Doubles Champion
Olympian in 2008

Killer: The opponent throws 10-15 shuttlecocks over the net. The player comes from the midcourt (center line) and jumps with a lunge (approximately from the front service line) into the net in order to hit the shuttle high over the net ('kill'). This should first be restricted to one half of the court. A variation is for the opponent to alternate between throwing to the player's backhand and forehand sides.

Drill 1: Short duel: Player A plays a dropshot from the back boundary line, player B pushes the shuttle back over the net, player A also returns with a short shot, as does B, then A hits the shuttle high to the back of the court and the drill starts again with a dropshot from B. The short game should feature spinning, lifting and slicing.

Drill 2: Sitting down game: Two players sit in the area of the front service line and play a rally composed of short shots.

Drill 3: Don't touch: A row of old shuttlecocks is placed feathers down along the top of the net. The player lunges from the midcourt toward the net and smashes the shuttles one after the other, making sure that he does not touch the net.

Drill 4: Net duel: Two players play a rally at the front of the court near the net until one of them makes a mistake, without killing the shuttlecock. The duel can be scored, in which case the front service line is the court boundary.

Drill 5: Screen: In order to reduce reaction time, towels are hung over the net as a screen. The two players now play a rally, but it is now more difficult for them to know where the other will hit the shuttlecock.

Fig. 78: It couldn't go any lower: Germany's Dieter Domke hits the shuttlecock just over the net.

14

Fig. 79: The muscular legs of two-time European women's champion Xu Huaiwen are the product of intensive running training.

14   Running Technique

Good running technique means that the player is able to **move as efficiently as possible** behind the shuttlecock and to return to the **base position** after the shot. Focusing on the central position is a crucial tactical element in badminton, particularly in the singles game. All the **corners of the court** are easy to reach from the center of the court, which means that it is the optimal position for the player to await his opponent's return shot. The running technique should therefore focus on allowing the player to return to this spot before the opponent can return the shuttlecock. Conversely, it is considered **good tactics** to force the opponent to run around the court, thus making it hard for him to return to the central position.

Fig. 80: The French player Pi Hongyan has an elegant running technique.

The running technique must be seen in conjunction with the hitting technique. The **running technique changes** according to the type of shot played. Leisure players often mistakenly think that badminton technique training only involves stroke practice, but badminton is a running-based sport, and players typically cover 2-3 miles during a match. Fast, coordinated footwork is required along with good basic fitness, and can be learnt by practicing the footwork without a shuttlecock. **Running and hitting techniques** should not be treated as separate entities.

While tall **Europeans** like the Danes and the English practiced the technique with rangy strides, the shorter Asians developed a type of play with short, quick strides culminating in a jump. Neither alternative is better than the other; it just depends on the player's physiology, and both types of play have influenced the development of the game. There are four basic types of special running technique that professional players have developed that have become more and more perfected over time, they are the **lunge, scissors jump, 'China' jump** and **jump smash**. However, the other strokes like the **clear, drop, smash, drive** and **backhand** also require special running techniques, which are dealt with in the relevant chapters of this book.

14.1 The Lunge

The **lunge** is a long-reaching step to the front, side or back. The step is so long that the **intermediate step is almost missing**. With the lunge, the player should reach and hit the shuttlecock simultaneously. However, the step should also be performed so that the player can return quickly to his original position and he must not get stuck in the lunge position, which can be done by ensuring that the **knee** of the lunging leg does not extend beyond the toes. The upper **body** should also remain as **upright as possible**, although this is not possible in every game situation. The **lunge step** sequence begins with a starting step, followed by an intermediate step with the left foot in order to move forward from the two-legged ready position. A lunging step toward the net with the right foot follows the starting step with the left foot.

Fig. 81: Lunge

In the lunge . . .

- Directly before the shot, the player performs a long, reaching step, usually into the far left or right of the forecourt.

- In the right forehand corner, the right leg is placed at the front, the left foot stays where it is to allow the player to move backward again more easily.

- In the left backhand corner, the left leg should move forward to allow the player to move back again more easily, although many textbooks state that if the right leg goes forward the body turns to the left, and it is harder to return to the ready position after a left-legged lunge.

- The player's forward movement stops suddenly.

- The right knee should not go beyond the ankle to make it easier for the player to return to the backward movement.

- The shuttlecock can be hit with the backhand or forehand.

14.2 The Scissors Jump

Fig. 82: The French player Pi Hongyan performs a scissors jump

The **scissors jump** is a **backwards running** technique in which the player hits the shuttlecock as he jumps backwards, which **saves the player a lot of time**, and means that he can start to run forward again straight afterwards. The hit-jump combination is performed so that the player takes his first step forwards as soon as he lands. The scissors jump is used for long shots that reach as far as the back boundary line. It is always an **overhead shot**, which can also be performed as a drop, clear or smash. As the player cannot hit as accurately in the air as when he is standing with two feet on the ground, it is hard to play a sensitive drop from this position.

In the scissors jump . . .

- The player hits the shuttlecock while moving backwards.

- The left hip moves forward first.

- The pelvis twists and the right hip pushes forward during the jump and hit.

- The shoulders also twist and the left elbow is pulled back and the right shoulder is moved forward during the jump and hit.

- The backwards jump ends on the left foot.

- The player can put his right foot forward straight after landing to initiate the forward movement.

- The left hand is raised for balance and aim during the jump.

Fig. 83: Scissors jump phase 1

Fig. 84: Scissors jump phase 2

Fig. 85: Scissors jump phase 3

Fig. 86: Scissors jump phase 4

14.3 The 'China' Jump

The **'China' jump** resembles the scissors jump in that the shuttlecock is hit during the **flight phase** (both feet in the air) while the player is moving backwards, Unlike the scissors jump though, the player does not just move backwards but right into the **rear corners of the court**. The right corner is easier to reach as a **round-the-head stroke** must be played from the left corner, which is a more complicated and therefore riskier stroke than the forehand overhead shot played from the right corner. In addition, the shuttle cannot be hit as hard from the left corner. When landing after the 'China' jump, the feet should also be one in front of the other to enable the player to **move forward** straight after landing. It is rarely possible to play a **sensitive dropshot** from a 'China' jump as accuracy is reduced during the jump.

In the 'China' jump . . .

* The player takes off with both feet.

* The player hits the shuttlecock while in the air.

* An overhead shot is always played.

* The player lands with both feet on the ground and with the bodyweight over the right or left foot, depending on whether he runs to the backhand or forehand corner.

* The upper body twists slightly.

* A forehand or backhand can be played parallel to the net.

* The shuttlecock can also be hit diagonally backwards or forwards.

Fig. 87: Judith Meulendijks from the Netherlands doing a China Jump

Fig. 88: 'China' jump phase 1

Fig. 89: 'China' jump phase 2

Fig. 90: 'China' jump phase 3

Fig. 91: 'China' jump phase 4

14.4 The Jump Smash

Fig. 92: 2003 World Champion Xia Xuanze from China, plays a jump smash

The **jump smash** is both very **effective** and **very tiring**. Jumping gives the shot a very **steep flight path**, which **reduces the opponent's reaction time**. However, the smash must be accurate and win the point, otherwise the player will soon get into trouble if the shuttle is unexpectedly returned by his opponent, and the player lands from the jump smash with both feet at the same time, which makes it **difficult for him to get to the center of the court** from the back boundary line.

The jump smash is one of the most **spectacular shots** in badminton due to its speed and power. It was the signature shot of the Indonesian **Liem Swie King**, who was a particularly good exponent of this shot at the start of the 80s. His countryman **Heryanto Arbi** (world champion in the mid-90s) followed in his footsteps and also deserves a mention, although severe **back problems** led to his premature retirement.

Fig. 93: The Danish player Peter Rasmussen plays a jump smash

In the jump smash . . .

- The player takes off with both feet.

- The shuttlecock is hit with full power.

- The player achieves a sharper angle for the smash.

- The player initially gives at the knees a little to gain momentum for the take off.

Drill 1: Shadow badminton: The correct jump movement sequence should be practiced. The player should stay briefly in the ready position and then perform the jump without a shuttlecock. After the jump the player returns immediately to the ready position.

Drill 2: Lunge: Boxes are placed in all four corners of one half of the court and a shuttlecock is placed on each box. The player runs from the ready position to one corner, takes a shuttlecock, returns to the ready position and then runs to the next corner and exchanges the shuttlecock.

Fig. 94: The Swede Elin Bergblom
signals the serve type.

15 Tactics (Singles, Doubles, Mixed)

15.1 Basic Tactical Rules

Tactics are an essential part of badminton along with **technique** and **fitness**. There are some basic tactical rules which apply to both the **women's and men's games** and **all disciplines**, and some tactical rules that differ greatly between singles, doubles and mixed doubles.

The main principle and **tactical guideline** in badminton is that the player should attempt **to reach every shot**. This not only corresponds to the idea of **fairness** but is an essential element of the sport itself. The player must have a **fighting mentality**. Resting on one's laurels during a game can quickly go wrong, as even big leads can be reversed within a few minutes. All it takes is a **brief lack** of concentration on the part of the leader. A player can also play **on a high** when he sees his shots are succeeding, particularly if he was not playing well before.

One of the tactical and technical principles is that the shuttlecock must be hit at the **highest point** so that the **shot is steep**, particularly in the case of the smash and the drop. It also shortens the **trajectory** of the shuttle. The further a shuttle travels, the **more quickly it loses speed**, so a short **trajectory reduces the opponent's reaction time**. Another reason for hitting the shuttle early is that shuttles hit from underneath are **defensive shots**, and they immediately put the player **under pressure**. Only by hitting the shuttle early can the player put his opponent under pressure.

Fig. 95: Olympic Champion Taufik Hidayat is an endurance type of player; he often plays long rallies.

When deciding on a tactical plan, the player should first focus on himself and the **strengths of his game**, and only then should he think about his opponent. Uppermost in his mind should be the **type of player** that he is, in terms of conditioning and technique: an **attacking player** (with powerful, well-placed shots) or a **defensive player** (good defense, hard-running, good shuttlecock control), an **endurance runner** (good fitness, accurate defensive strokes) or a **technical player** (well-placed shots, short rallies). Of course, players should aim to have all these qualities, but a player who is aware of his strengths and can therefore **bring calm and consistency** to his game, is able to go into a match with **plenty of confidence**.

Fig. 96: Juliane Schenk talks tactics with coach Jeroen van Dijk.

Tactics should be developed to suit the above-mentioned player types. Every player's aim should be to **control the game**. A game can be made faster or slower, depending on the opponent's ability and resistance. The **single's player** should aim to return to the **center of the court** after every rally, because all four corners of the court are equally accessible from this position. To read more about the central, or base, position, please also see Chapter 4, "The Ready Position".

In the **doubles discipline**, the main tactical aim should be an **understanding between the players**. They should be able to trust each other blindly and know each other's running paths. They should be clear about which player is responsible for hitting the shuttlecock in which situations; this is something that can be learnt by intensive **match practice in training**. Any **misunderstandings and disagreements** should be **analyzed and talked** through immediately.

The same rules apply for the **mixed doubles**, although in many mixed couples, the **woman covers the net** and **the man tends to cover the back of the court**, because his physique allows him to hit more powerful attacking shots.

Fig. 97: Fighting for every point is one of the basic tactical rules of badminton.

General tactical rules include . . .

- Every point should be fought for, regardless of the score (points can only be won by making the opponent move).

- The opponent must be made to run (this is best done by hitting to all four corners of the court in no particular order).

- Players should only use strokes that they can play well (don't take unnecessary risks).

- Exploit the opponent's weaknesses; the shuttlecock should be hit so that it is as hard as possible for the opponent to return it (e.g. hit at the body if the opponent is tall).

- The game is speeded up; the player tries to get to the shuttlecock as early as possible.

- The player shouldn't allow himself to be ruffled (bad calls by the umpire, noisy spectators or provocation by the opponent should be ignored).

- The player should concentrate before starting a rally (breathe in before serving).

- The player should focus on his strengths (don't dwell on shots that have gone wrong).

- The player shouldn't show any emotion to his opponent (this could give him confidence unnecessarily).

- The player should avoid turning his back to the net wherever possible, thus losing sight of the shuttlecock and his opponent (this means avoiding the backhand overhand stroke, use a round-the-head stroke instead).

- Don't be too quick to change tactics once they are decided.

- Don't play strokes that the opponent can reach easily (diagonal shots can often be 'read' and therefore exploited by the opponent; so play down the line instead of cross-court).

- Keep your eye on the shuttlecock (this will stop you from being influenced by the opponent's feints).

- Vary types of serve.

- Vary the tempo (don't just attack relentlessly, but also include drops, flicks or net play).

- Use feints (physical movements and even the direction of gaze send signals to the opponent which deceive him as to the actual shot to be played).

- Try to avoid playing defensively in order to dictate the game.

- The shuttlecock should always be hit at the highest point, in front of the body.

Fig. 98: Players should not let themselves get riled by the umpire's decisions. Dutch player Judith Meulendijks lets her temperament get the better of her here.

Tip: Feint practice should be incorporated into training, i.e. deceiving the opponent with regard to the direction or power of the shot. For example, one could pretend to be preparing a gentle, sensitive serve but at the last minute actually play a powerful one. A great deal of concentration is required when looking in one direction and then hitting it in a different direction.

The tactical principles for each discipline are analyzed and described in more detail on the following pages.

15.2 Singles Tactics

In the singles, the aim should be to force the opponent away from the **base position**. The best way to do this is to hit very accurately to **the four corners of the court** so that the opponent is constantly on the move. In the singles, the player tries if possible to return to the base position after every shot if possible (see chapter 4 "The Ready Position"), from where he can reach all four corners of the court equally easily. This is exactly why it makes sense to try to stop the opponent from reaching the shuttlecock quickly and **preparing well for the return**.

Already **when serving**, the player should follow the tactics of playing **to the far corners** of the court by serving into the left or right corners. The shuttlecock lands just behind the opponent's service line. Alternatively, hit to the two corners at the back of the court, either with a **long, high serve** or a **flick serve**. As the flick must be performed very quickly, there is a high risk that it will land 'out'. The serve should be **varied as much as possible** so that the opponent cannot guess which serve is coming next.

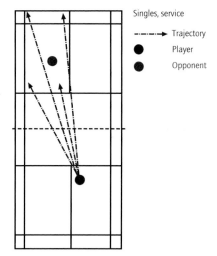

Singles, service

---·-·-·▸ Trajectory

● Player

● Opponent

In elite badminton, all serves in singles tend to be **backhands**, as the short backswing makes it hard for the opponent to know if to expect a short or long serve. However, the serve should be played **more often to the back boundary line** at the back of the court than short to the service line, as this makes the opponent run further and forces him to hit the shuttlecock from an **unfavorable position**.

When **receiving serve**, the player should stand as far as possible along the center line to cover his backhand. The **racket is raised** when waiting for the serve in order to

Fig. 99: The Chinese player Xie Xingfang preparing to play a forehand serve.

be able to kill a short shot if necessary, although it is one of the basic principles of badminton to hit the shuttlecock as high as possible.

Individual physical, motor and mental qualities are very important in singles. Is the player's main strength his technique, conditioning or creativity? Players can be roughly divided into two categories: **attacking and defensive players**. A player should know which type he belongs to, as this determines how he trains and how he plays in matches.

The **attacking player** has a **powerful game** and is usually very good at getting to the shuttlecock and hitting it **very early**. He should be able to **hit hard** and have a **good technique**. His game is also characterized by its **speed and speed strength**, and his use of **feints**. The tactical approach is to **reduce long rallies** to a minimum as this is very tiring.

The **defensive player** must have **excellent endurance abilities** in order to cope with many long rallies. His tactic is to **wear his opponent** down until he is exhausted. This strategy allows players who are **weaker technically** to compensate for this shortcoming. As well as **good conditioning**, they should be **mentally prepared** to keep their concentration for long periods. They must also keep their cool throughout long rallies and **await their chance**, or their opponent's errors, during long duels. They should be **proficient in the smash defense**, in particular.

Single tactics include . . .

- The player waits for the opponent's shots in the center of the court (on the center line, about 1 yard behind the service line).

- The shuttlecock should be hit so that the player has enough time to return to the base position.

- The player serves from near the center line (the left foot is almost touching the service line in the forehand serve and the right foot in the backhand).

- The long serve should land as close as possible to the central line (this forces the opponent to play a diagonal return, possibly within the player's reach).

- Don't smash from the back boundary line (the shuttlecock quickly loses speed and is traveling relatively slowly when it reaches the opponent, the shuttlecock must be also hit very high and hard in order to get the right angle to the net).

- Smashes are played from the midcourt.

- The player's position in relation to the shuttlecock is correct.

- When serving, the player doesn't stand right at the front on the service line but a little further back (unlike in doubles, the back boundary line is the service line and the player must therefore cover a bigger court area).

- Sometimes playing a delaying strategy in order to tire the opponent out (i.e. playing neither attacking nor defensive shots in order to extend rallies).

15.3 Doubles Tactics

In a doubles pairing, each player must only cover **one half of the court**, unlike the singles, thus enabling players to **reach the shuttlecock more quickly** and often making **rallies faster**. Players must also have very **quick reactions** and understand each other very well so that each player knows which part of the court the other is responsible for. The following descriptions mainly apply to men's doubles, the specific demands of women's and mixed doubles are described elsewhere.

As in singles, the **service** should be played to **all four corners** of the opponent's court, as these are the **hardest places** for the opponent **to return** the shuttlecock from, thus forcing him to play defensive shots. Note that the court dimensions are different in doubles than in singles though: the **court is wider and shorter** (as in doubles the front long service line is used). This has tactical implications, because the shortness of the court means that the long serve must be played shorter, which usually enables the opponent to return it as an attacking shot. The less accurately the serve is hit, the easier it is for the opponent to do this.

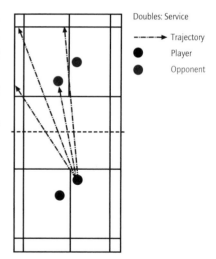

Doubles: Service

--·--·--▶ Trajectory
● Player
● Opponent

This is why **serves** are usually played **short in doubles**; this is the best way to put the opponent on the **defensive**. However, the odd long serve should still be included occasionally so that the opponent is **never quite sure** which serve to expect. A **flick serve** would be perfect here. The server stands in the front corner of his service court near the **t-junction**, and the partner stands slightly further back, but already in the **attacking formation**, even during the serve, for the server stands nearer the front of the court and concentrates on covering the net area and the partner covers the back of the court.

The serve-receivers also **stand slightly offset one in front of the other** and are also ready to attack. The serve receiver stands right at the front of the court at the t-junction so that he is **ready to lunge** forward to kill an overly short serve. Both the server and serve receiver are therefore **trying to attack.** This is the nature of the doubles game: to attack as quickly and as often as possible.

Doubles can be roughly divided into two situations: attack and defense, with a very **rapid transition** between the two. In doubles the partners move around each other like the ends of a **compass needle**, they turn around an imaginary center. When playing defensively they **stand next to each other**, and the player on the left covers the center of the court if he is right-handed. When attacking, one player **stands in front of the other**, and for tactical reasons, **slightly offset**, so that if the back player smashes from the right forehand corner, the front player stands on the left side of the court at the net, thus covering the corner furthest away from his partner.

Fig. 100: Doubles tactics include letting your partner know which serve to expect, as demonstrated by Juliane Schenk.

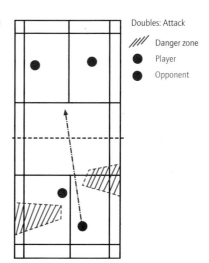

Doubles: Attack

//// Danger zone

● Player

● Opponent

Fig. 101: The Korean Jung Jae-Sung and Lee Young-Dae on the attack. One pops the shuttlecock over the net and the other covers the back of the court.

As already mentioned, doubles partners stand behind one another when attacking. By playing **smashes and drops**, the rear player tries to force the opponent to play **weak defensive shots** so that they can be 'killed' by his partner, who covers the front of the court and waits for the opponents' **short defensive returns**. The attacking team should aim mainly for the boundary lines and down the centerline as these areas are hardest for the opponents to defend. The attacking team should strive to **put as much pressure as possible** on their opponents and not relax until they have won the point. Clears should therefore be avoided. The **danger zone** that attacking players find most difficult to defend is the **area behind the head of the front player and at the sidelines**, because this is where the areas of **responsibility of both players overlap** and it is not clear who should play the shot. This can be overcome to some extent by **specific training and good communication** between the partners.

The defending team should aim to stop playing defensively and **start attacking**. The partners stand approximately side-by-side and **cover one side of the court each**. The best way to do this is to play several **flat shots** down the opponents' sidelines and to **avoid hitting across the center** of the court. **Defensive clears** should reach the opponents' **rear boundary line** to make it as difficult as possible for the opponent to play a smash.

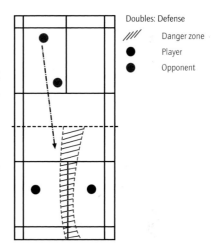

Doubles: Defense

//// Danger zone
● Player
● Opponent

Doubles players should be particularly careful about **defending the central area** of their own court as this is the hardest area to defend. The opponents should **aim to attack** here as this is where the areas of responsibility of both partners overlap and there is **sometimes confusion** as to who should return the shot. However the unwritten rule is that **forehand takes precedence over backhand**, i.e. the player on the left covers the central area as he can usually hit harder and more accurately with his forehand. The front player's **racket should always be raised** so that he can reach the shuttlecock quickly. He should be just as active as the back player, and he should run back and forth with his **knees slightly bent**, forming a diagonal with the back player.

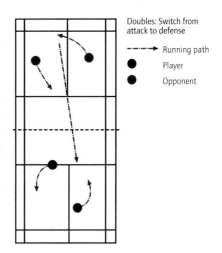

Doubles: Switch from attack to defense

-·-·-·➤ Running path
● Player
● Opponent

Fig. 102: The Malaysian duo Wong Pei Tty and Chin Eei Hui stand side by side waiting for their opponents to attack.

Fig. 103: The Malaysians are now attacking and stand slightly offset one behind the other.

Teams are constantly **switching between attacking and defending** during a game and the **transitions are very quick**. When the attacking players botch an attack or the opponents are able to go on the offensive due to a well-placed shot, the players must switch as quickly as possible to the defensive formation. This means no longer **standing one behind the other** but moving in a **clockwise direction** to **stand side by side** in order to **cover one side of the court each**. The player who was at the front now moves to the left side of the court and the other partner moves from behind to the right side of the court. The players only run in the opposite direction in exceptional cases, as it gives them further to run.

The players should also move in a **clockwise direction** when **switching from defensive to attacking formations**. The player on the right moves up to the net while the player on the left moves to the back of the court and puts pressure on the opponents with attacking shots. The players move around each other switching from attacking to defensive formations like a **compass needle**. The image of a compass needle is also appropriate because the players form **a diagonal line through the imaginary mid-point** of the court. In the attacking formation, this means that if the back player smashes from the right from his forehand corner, the partner stands front left, enabling him to cover the part of the court furthest from his partner.

Fig. 104: Denmark's Lars Paaske and Jonas Rasmussen await the opponent's return standing one behind the other in an attacking formation.

95

The tactics described above apply both for men's and **women's doubles**, but **defensive play is particularly important** in the women's game as they **are not as powerful or fast** as the men. There are often long rallies that cannot be finished off with a powerful, well-placed smash. The points must be prepared very well beforehand by the women. They should therefore be ready to ruthlessly exploit weak returns from their opponents. Many points are won by **capitalizing on weak shots**. The aim is to force the opponents to make mistakes and exploit them by **playing variations of flick serves, dropshots and clears**.

Doubles tactics include . . .

- Faster and more aggressive play than in singles (two players cover the court better than one as they can reach the shuttlecock more quickly).

- A good understanding between the partners as to which area each player is responsible for.

- The server signaling to his partner which type of serve he is going to play (this can be done verbally or by sign language).

- The importance of the serve and reception of serve (many rallies are over with the first return).

- Almost only playing short serves in order to force the opponent to hit the shot high and out.

- The serving pair standing quite closely one behind the other (the back player waits for the high return and can attack; already when serving they adopt an attacking formation).

- The attacking pair are slightly offset (the front player always moves diagonally to the back player and covers the net area, while the back player puts pressure on the opponents with smashes and dropshots).

- The front player in an attacking pair holds his racket high so as to be ready to hit immediately when the shuttlecock enters his territory.

- The defending pair stand side by side (the player on the left takes care of shots down the center with his forehand).

- The defending pair tries to return to the offensive (the best way to do this is with a flat defensive shot down the side tramlines).

Fig. 105: In the mixed doubles, the woman always stands to the left of the man when he is serving, as demonstrated by the Polish couple Robert Mateusiak and Nadiezda Kostiuczyk.

15.4 Mixed Doubles Tactics

Mixed doubles tactics should reflect the **different physical attributes of men and women**. Compared to women, men can usually **hit harder** and have **superior speed-strength**. This should be incorporated into the tactical game plan. The **man** is therefore better employed **covering the back of the court** and in an attacking situation puts pressure on the opponents by playing smashes and dropshots. The **woman covers the front right of the court**.

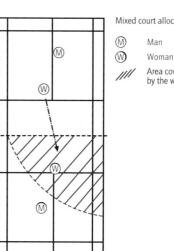

Mixed court allocation

Ⓜ Man
Ⓦ Woman
/// Area covered by the woman

Fig. 106: Attack in mixed doubles

Fig. 107: Defense in mixed doubles

Right from the **start of the game**, the woman should stand at the front of the court on the service line, whether she herself or her partner is serving. The **woman** therefore always **stands slightly in front of the man**, which allows her to run back to the net after serving to cover her area. The service target areas are the same as for the men's doubles as described above, but when the woman (and also the man) serves, she should not be afraid to play **many short serves**, as they could be 'killed' very powerfully if she hits them too high. When serving to a woman, a **flick serve** is often used as it forces the woman to run backwards. The partner is also forced to hit the shuttlecock at the front of the court, so that both partners are then playing in **tactically unwise positions**. In this situation, the woman should either play a smash or a drop and try to get up to the net again so that her partner can move to the back of the court.

If both partners are equally good, the **defensive formations** are side by side, the same as in the men's doubles. Alternatively, the partners can **play defensively from slightly offset positions**, with the **woman moving** along the service line at the front of the court and **diagonally to the attacking man** on the opposite side of the court. This allows her to counter **diagonal smashes or dropshots** with net shots, while her partner can wait for a drive or a clear at **the back of the court**.

Mixed doubles tactics . . .

- Tactics are the same as for doubles (in particular if the man and woman are equally strong players).

- When attacking, the man should try to stand behind the woman (physical differences mean that the man can usually hit faster and harder).

- When the man is serving, the woman stands as far forward as possible on the center line (the woman cannot get to the net so quickly and the man takes up the attacking position at the back).

- More flick serves are played to the woman.

- In a defensive formation, the man stand slightly offset at the back and covers the tramlines and the woman covers the diagonal area.

- The woman always stands to the left of the man when he is serving.

16

Fig. 108: Peak performances, such as this by Pi Hongyan, cannot be achieved throughout the year, which is why training should be periodized.

16 Training

The foundations for a successful tournament are laid in training. A player's performance can be improved by means of **clever planning** and **regular practice**. Players of any age can improve thanks to the **body's adaptation mechanisms**, i.e. by **setting appropriate physical stimuli** in training. It is a good idea to **analyze and log training and competition performances** in order to have objective criteria with which to **plan a training program** and **monitor performance**.

The **components of sports performance** include the following areas:

* technique (stroke and running technique).

* tactics.

* conditioning (endurance, strength, speed, coordination).

* mind (mental training).

This chapter deals both with **training periodization** and **structure** and the areas of **conditioning and mental training**. **Technique** and **tactics** are dealt with in other chapters.

An optimal combination of **loading and rest** produces a **training effect**. This applies both to a single workout and the year-long training program. Training loads the whole **body** (cardiovascular system, nervous system, muscles and glands). Training is **tiring**, but players always **recover**, quickly or slowly depending on their physical constitution.

Particularly in the area of **conditioning**, a so-called **supercompensation effect** occurs, which means that the player not only recovers his original performance level, but by repeating the workout actually improves his performance level. If the **recovery phases are too short**, at some point the body will become **overloaded** and suffer from burnout, and the performance level will fall to below the starting level. Excessive recovery periods between workouts mean that the supercompensation effect is lost.

The intensity of **hitting and running drills** can be **increased** by only allowing the player to use a reduced number of strokes or only using one part of the court.

In general, **training goals** should **not be set too high**. The aims must be achievable, otherwise players will become **frustrated** and lose confidence.

16.1 Periodization

The training sessions should be part of a **long-term training program**, which is geared towards peak performances. Training is **periodized**, because it is wise to vary the loading on the body to give it the **chance to regenerate** in order to avoid chronic overtraining and a drop in performance. Periodization is mainly **oriented around tournaments** and can roughly be divided into three phases: the **preparation phase** (usually in the summer months before the start of the competitive season), the **competition phase** (September to March) and the **transition phase** (April to July).

The training emphasis in the **preparation phase** is on **fitness**, and the physical foundations for competitions and training are laid by working on **strength, endurance and speed**. The body is **often exhausted** during this stage and the performance level drops.

In the **competition phase**, the player works on his **technique and tactics**, and it features individual **stroke drills** or **match practice**. Before a tournament (league game with the team or ranking list tournament) the player should allow sufficient time for regeneration. A day of rest should follow a hard training session before a competition, otherwise the player will go into the tournament with tired legs. Conditioning training should also be reduced in this phase as regular competition provides a workout and the body needs to rest.

The **transition phase** is intended to be a phase of **active recovery** in which the body regenerates from its previous exertions. It is a very good idea to put aside the badminton racket for a couple of weeks and to keep fit by **practicing other sports**, e.g. jogging, swimming, cycling or basketball. It is counterproductive to try to maintain the same high performance level year-round, as this will lead to exhaustion and **overtraining** in the long term which will severely affect performance levels. The body has its limits and **injury** will be the result.

16.2 How to Structure a Training Session

At first we should decide on the **scheduling** and **contents of a training session**. A training session should, irrespective of the performance level, always be divided into **three phases of differing lengths**. A 90-minute workout, for example, would go like this:

a) **Warm-up** (10 mins): The player warms up without racket and shuttlecock by performing running and stretching exercises or by playing warm-up games if desired, in order to raise the body temperature to the right level.

b) **Main part** (60 mins): This section starts with a few short, relaxed hits of the shuttlecock ("knocking up"), followed by specific drills to improve running and hitting techniques and tactics, the intensity is high and rest breaks are short.

c) **Final part** (20 mins): Depending on the time of year and player's fitness, conditioning (circuit) training or a ball game such as basketball can now be carried out to improve coordination. This phase is usually reserved for match practice though; the training focus of the main part of the workout is used in a game played for points. The final section should always conclude with stretching in order to reduce the risk of injury; the body is slowly returned to a resting state again.

A basic rule is that a training **session should be varied** and contain **different intensity** levels. The player should constantly **set new mental and physical stimuli** in order to improve. An interesting workout should **keep the player motivated**, help him to withstand the loading and keep training enjoyable.

The **size of the training group** determines the organization of hitting and running training. One coach can usually look after up to 8 players on a court, but the ideal number is 1-4.

Fig. 109: Every training session should include a warm-up and stretching.

Here are some suitable drills, ordered according to the number of participants:

a) **One player.** Shuttle machine: The coach has a large box of shuttles and hits them in quick succession to predetermined parts of the court so that the player can practice individual strokes and running paths.

Police Game: The coach points with his hand or racket to certain corners of the court, thereby directing the player around the court.

b) **Two players.** The players decide to play on either a whole or half court, and play e.g. dropshot rallies. This drill is particularly useful if the players are of equal ability and any combination of strokes can be practiced. The 1 on 1 game is the most effective form of training. Alternatively, the coach can work with one player as in a) above while the other player rests.

c) **Three players.** The players can train in pairs as in b) above, while the other player rests. Alternatively, they can practice 2 against 1, which places the lone player under pressure as he has to cover the same court area as his two opponents and is therefore appropriate if a stronger player is training with two weaker players. If all players are equally good, the players can change around so that each one plays alone for a while. For example, they can agree that once the lone player has made 10 mistakes he changes to play in a pair. This enables each player to determine how long or how hard he trains.

d) **Four players.** To make training as intensive as possible, the players should train in pairs on half a court, and players of equal ability should train together where possible. If there are doubles players in the group, then this formation allows doubles game situations to be practiced (e.g. the switch between attacking and defensive formations).

e) **Five to eight players.** Such a large training group is only really a good idea for beginners as the drills intensity is too low. Either four players can practice on the court as in d) above, while the others rest, or they can play a run-around, where the training group is divided into two halves, standing on either side of the net. The players take turns in hitting the shuttle and then run around to the other side of the court and stand in line waiting to hit the shuttle again. A variation of this could be that players are out of the game if they make three mistakes and the drill continues until only two players are left and they play off for the best of five points.

16.3 Performance Monitoring

Performance tests allow the player to check whether or not he is meeting his **training goals**. Tests can be used to measure both **fitness** and **technique**. The tests should be **quick and efficient** so that they don't disturb training too much. It is important to use comparable values to **give clear results**.

Physical loading can be measured by the **pulse rate**, which should be interpreted according to **age and gender**. Training condition, **health, time of day and climatic conditions** also affect the result.

The pulse should be measured with the **index finger on the inside of the wrist** or the **carotid artery**. It is sufficient to take the pulse for only 15 seconds, and to multiply the number of beats by four to obtain the usual **value of one minute**. Heart rate monitors that **measure the pulse or heart rate** can be purchased for around $ 30 and can be worn throughout training to allow the player to check his pulse rate quickly.

Elite players have a resting pulse rate of around 50 bpm or even less, while for untrained players this value is 70 bpm or more. After heavy workouts the pulse rate of very **fit players can rise to around 150 bpm**. The fitter the player, the quicker the player recovers from the loading and the quicker **the pulse rate drops**. If the pulse rate only drops slowly, this indicates that the **body is overloaded**. A pale face or feelings of dizziness also indicate overtraining.

Tip: To measure the players' performance level, the pulse should be measured twice, the second time shortly after the first. The first measurement should be taken directly after an exhausting drill, and the second three minutes later. The pulse should now be below 120 bpm in order to be able to move onto the next drill.

Conditioning levels can be measured by how **many repetitions** a player can complete in a certain time. Badminton-appropriate examples are jumping rope or push-ups. A very good way to monitor performance is by means of a **training circuit** that includes **drills for speed strength, strength endurance and jumping power**. The number of repetitions accomplished should be entered in the training log and then used to compare with results from the same workout repeated on other occasions.

Make sure that the **drills in training circuits** or performance tests do not exceed 2 minutes to **simulate the loading intensity of a game** of badminton. Individual rallies **seldom last longer than 2 minutes**.

It is more **difficult to monitor the technical and running abilities** of a badminton player than his physical fitness, as it is very dependent on the judgment of the coach who evaluates the performance. The player should be **constantly working on each stroke** (drop, clear, smash, flick, drive, serve and net play) separately in training. From a very young age, Asian players perform a kind of drill training for each stroke separately **to increase stroke confidence**.

To gain an overview of **training volume and intensity** and **ultimately performance**, the ambitious player should keep **a daily training log**. This should be checked regularly (once a week if the player trains every day), as it is used to determine training content and volume for the following week.

The following should be noted in the training diary . . .

- resting pulse rate in the morning before getting up

- weight (once or twice a week)

- training content (type, duration)

- other activities (massage, gymnastics, sauna, swimming, etc.)

- performance-diminishing factors (illness, injury, professional or personal problems)

This overview allows the player to monitor the training actually performed and to see the correlation between loading, performance improvement, fatigue, regeneration and possible overtraining. The player will gradually start to see when and how he can produce a peak performance, because the long-term connections between intensity and performance will become clear.

16.4 Conditioning

Conditioning is the foundation for a sport like badminton that **involves a lot of running**. Achievement-oriented players should mainly work on their fitness **in the preparation phase** (see Chapter 16.1 "Periodization"). Don't forget that badminton also involves a lot of short bursts of speed and short breaks. **Conditioning training** should therefore predominantly be **interval training** in which the player **alternates between loading and rest**. Conditioning can be divided into **endurance, strength, speed and agility**, and should include drills to improve all of these areas.

The endurance area is further subdivided into **aerobic and anaerobic endurance**, according to the method of **energy supply to the body**. The aerobic method involves the **burning of glucose and fatty acids**, and this process requires oxygen so that the endurance level depends on the efficiency of the cardiovascular system. Aerobic endurance can be improved by targeted endurance training.

In the **anaerobic process**, the burning of energy provided by the body is not sufficient; it must be obtained by **oxidative processes**. The body gets down to the nitty-gritty as it were, and

Fig. 110: Badminton is very running-intensive, as demonstrated here by Juliane Schenk.

goes into **lactate deficit**. The body reacts to longer periods of anaerobic loading with a **rapid drop in performance**. As a badminton match can last up to one and a half hours, and most of this time is spent running intensively, even the fittest players play in the anaerobic area.

As badminton consists of many **quick movements**, training should focus on speed **strength and strength endurance** as well as agility. Speed strength involves performing certain movements as fast as possible, whereas strength endurance involves maintaining the exertion of strength for as long as possible. Unlike bodybuilders, for example, who try to lift the heaviest weights possible, **maximal strength** has very little relevance in badminton. When training in the gym, badminton players should predominantly perform many repetitions with light weights.

General endurance (aerobic and anaerobic) is trained by . . .

- Endurance running (not less than 30 minutes) over varied terrain so that the running speed changes. Every 10 minutes, perform a speed-strength or plyometric drill so as not to make it an exclusively long endurance workout.
- Cycling outside or on the exercise bike (varying the intensity).

Strength (speed strength and strength endurance) are trained by . . .

- Dumbbell training (light weights and high reps)
- Jumping rope
- Circuit training (drills for legs, abs, arms, chest, shoulders and back), e.g. sit-ups, chin-ups, push-ups, medicine ball throws
- Plyometric drills

Speed is trained by . . .

- Jumping rope
- Plyometric drills (hurdles, pop-ups, squat jumps, astride jumps, etc.)
- Sprints (short distances up 22 yards)
- Shadow badminton (running training without a shuttle)

Coordination and agility are trained by . . .

- Shadow badminton
- Complex badminton drills
- Juggling
- Shots with a basketball

Drill 1: Jumping rope (double jumps), as performed by the Indonesians in training. The drill lasts about 32 minutes. Step 1: 45 seconds skipping, 15 seconds rest (20 reps); Step 2: 30 seconds skipping, 15 seconds rest (15 reps); Step 3: 15 seconds skipping, 15 seconds rest (10 reps).

Drill 2: Lap running: the player runs for 15 minutes around a 440 yard track and counts how many laps he is able to complete. This result is used to measure the player's aerobic endurance (VO_2 max).

Drill 3: Medicine Ball throw: two players sit facing each other and throw a medicine back and forth between them. The ball is taken behind the head and thrown to the opposite player. Rest after every 15 throws (strength endurance).

16.5 Mental Training

The term **mental training** was coined in **Sports Psychology** and refers to the repeated **visualization or mental practice of an action**, without actively performing the action. The knowledge and methods have their origin in **behavioral therapy** and have been adapted to the requirements of sports psychology.

Fig. 111: The Dane Peter Gade has often suffered from nerves during his career.

Sports psychologists have been used in elite level badminton for **just a few years**. Players like the many-time Danish European Champion **Peter Gade** have turned to a psychologist after suffering from mental problems. The Dane was repeatedly considered to be the favorite in big tournaments, but was often affected by nerves. In critical game situations he **bottled out**, and was unable to play at his best. He wanted to call the opponent's shots out and did not return the shuttlecock, even though he could have hit them. All too often they landed in the court though, allowing the opponent to score a few points. Gade tried to **change this negative experience pattern** by using mental training.

An improvement in the action in the conscious, **intensive visualization** should cause an **improvement in the action** when it is actually performed. The realized effect depends on how vividly the visualization succeeds, i.e. how successfully and realistically it simulates the action and how sensitive it is to the internal processes involved. This requires a constant **switching between mental training and actual training**, so that the action in the visualization can be repeatedly compared to the performed action.

It is essential that training not only engage the **mind** but also the **body**. Both **must work in harmony** so that their powers can be focused and deployed towards the same goal. This holistic approach is also reflected in the techniques that are used in mental training. Which techniques are used depends on various factors: the training emphasis, the coach's method preference and the player's starting situation and goals. It usually consists of a combination of:

• concentration and relaxation exercises

• autogenic training

• introduction to positive thinking

• meditation

• a guide to visualization

Fig. 112: Positive thinking is best reinforced by remembered successes. Here the English mixed doubles pair Nathan Robertson and Gail Emms celebrate their World Championships victory in 2006.

Fig. 113: In mental training, players are encouraged to remember positive experiences. Here Denmark's Peter Rasmussen celebrates a victory.

Autogenic training is a **relaxation method** that is **based on autosuggestion** that is also very helpful for badminton players. The Berlin psychiatrist Johannes Heinrich Schultz **developed it from hypnosis** and first published it in the book "Autogenic Training" in 1932. The prerequisite is a **calm body** in which the muscles can **completely relax**. The exercises consist of short, formulaic visualizations that the player must mentally focus on many times over. The simple version of autogenic training consists of seven exercises that are usually done consecutively.

Exercise 1: The calming exercise constitutes the introduction. It is used to relax and improve concentration. Shut your eyes and mentally repeat the sentence: "I am completely calm and nothing can bother me."

Exercise 2: The heaviness exercise can, after plenty of training, trigger a feeling of heaviness in the desired parts of the body. Say to yourself: "My arms and legs are heavy."

Exercise 3: The warmth exercise boosts blood circulation in the extremities. Say to yourself: "My arms and legs feel warm."

Exercise 4: The breathing exercise increases relaxation via a conscious breathing technique. Say to yourself: "My breath is flowing calmly and evenly." Don't deliberately inhale and exhale longer though. Let your breathing follow the natural rhythm of your body and it will calm down by itself.

Exercise 5: The heart exercise involves concentrating on the heartbeat. Imagine the sentence: My heart is beating calmly and regularly." Never say: "My heart is beating slowly." In extreme cases this can lead to cardiac irregularity.

Exercise 6: The solar plexus exercise focuses on the center of the abdomen. Say to yourself: "My abdomen is flowing with warmth."

Exercise 7: The head exercise helps to maintain alertness and improve concentration. Say to yourself: "My head is clear, my brain is cool."

Last but not least say once to yourself emphatically: "Arms firm! Take a deep breath! Eyes up!" Stretching brings the exercise phase to a close. The recovery phase is vital in order to come out of the trancelike state.

As well as relaxation, which can also be achieved with Yoga, the main focus of mental training is positive thinking.

Tips from the Pros:

Fig. 114: Detlef Poste

Detlef Poste
Born 1966
Head National Coach, Germany 2005-2008
German Men's Singles Champion 1992
German Badminton Association Director since 2009

Mental preparation: Every player's pre-match warm-up is different. Some run though moves once in their heads, then run through these actions in shadow badminton. Others think less specifically, and just try to relax as much as possible. For me, and for many other players with whom I have worked, it has always been important that before focusing on tactics, to pay attention to the basics (waiting calmly for shots, quick landing in the corner, loose racket grip until just before playing a stroke). Only when these basics are in place can one reach the shuttlecock quickly and early and put tactics into practice.

Fig. 115: On the podium at the Olympic Games in Athens.

17 The Competition

Competition day requires **specific preparation**. The match does not start when the players enter the court. As well as the specific match preparations, the general conditions must also be right.

Competition conditions include . . .

- Sufficient sleep (not too much and not too little).

- Eat and drink right (have sufficient water available and drink it regularly on competition day; bananas are the most suitable food).

- Prompt arrival at the court before the game (at least 30 minutes before the start).

Specific match preparation includes . . .

- If possible, studying the opponent's game (analysis of his strengths and weaknesses); in long waiting times during a competition. Practice this analysis by studying the playing style of any player.

- Knowing one's own strengths, and what the tactical implications are of this.

- Warming-up (loose running and stretching exercises, particularly for arm and shoulder muscles).

- Knocking up (at least 5 minutes, starting with clears, then drops, flat shots and short shots, finally a couple of serves).

Tips from the Pros:

Fig. 116: Jeroen van Dijk

Jeroen van Dijk
Born 1971
Six-time Dutch Singles Champion, since 2005 member of the German Badminton Association coaching staff, since 2008 German event coach for Men's Singles. He guided Xu Huaiwen to two European Championships titles.

Have the right attitude towards your opponent: first, know what kind of player your opponent is; is he normally a stronger, equal or weaker player than you? If the opponent is a lot stronger, a player can play freely. He should not put himself under pressure by trying to win points by playing difficult shots. An opponent of similar ability is the most difficult type of opponent. Mistakes are unavoidable and should not be dwelled on; instead the player should concentrate on fighting for every point. When playing a weaker opponent, it is important for the player to dictate the game and not to give the opponent any chances. In all three cases, in the last 15 minutes before the game starts, the players should go over his tactics, get into a positive frame of mind and approach the fight with his opponent positively.

Fig. 117: The Dane Camilla Martin has escaped serious injury during her career.

18 Injury Risk and Prevention (Warm-Up)

The **risk of injury** is generally considered **to be low** in badminton, almost certainly due to the fact that there is **no physical contact with the opponent(s)**. However, badminton is **characterized by very quick footwork, explosive strokes and reflexes**, all of which put **great strain on the tendons and ligaments**. The most frequent types of injury are therefore **sprained ligaments, muscle fiber tears, sprained ankle or** occasionally also a **torn ligament**. An **Achilles tendon tear** is particularly serious and takes months to heal. This **long break from training** and the **psychological recovery** from the accident mean that a return to former playing levels is slow and gradual.

A **sprained ankle**, i.e. the hyperextension of the joint capsule, **must be treated promptly**. A pressure bandage, which must be applied not more than **3 minutes after the accident**, can stop internal bleeding thus shortening healing time. The foot should then **be iced and raised**. A sprain causes the affected area to **swell, the bruising turns the area blue and it hurts. Medical attention** must always be sought,

115

which is also the case for minor ligament injuries. A succession of minor joint injuries can lead to **arthrosis**, even in younger players.

Fig. 118: The Dane Tine Rasmussen suffered an Achilles tendon tear in 2005. Two years later she won the All England Open.

An **Achilles tendon tear** usually happens without warning and the tendon **suddenly rips with a loud crack**. Tendon tears are usually caused by incorrect loading or overloading of the tendon, not by an inadequate pre-match warm-up (this only applies to ligaments). After the tear, the player doesn't usually feel any pain and **must be taken to hospital immediately**. There is no point in attempting alternative treatment at the court. The rupture can be treated surgically with an operation or conservatively with firm taping. The healed Achilles tendon, like all other ruptured tendons, **will never regain all of its former resilience**, which even in the best-case scenarios will be 80-90 % of that of a healthy tendon. 30 years ago, such a serious injury meant the end of the affected player's career at the highest level, but in recent years, players like the Dane Tine Rasmussen and the German record national player Nicole Grether have achieved world class performances following tendon ruptures.

Players who have a tendency to twist their **ankles should tape** the joint for extra stability. Badminton players should also **wear the correct flat gym shoes**, which aid ankle stability. For the treatment of slight tears and muscle tension, some players apply the new **Kinesio®tape**, created in Japan.

Unusual injury: once in a badminton training session, a small screw from the cork base of the shuttlecock flew into the eye of a Chinese squad player. The base had become dislodged after a very powerful shot from his partner.

To avoid injuries, the badminton player should **warm up for several minutes** before each game. The **muscles and ligaments** are raised to the correct operating temperature by means of **running and stretching exercises**, focusing on areas that are particularly important in badminton such as the **legs, shoulders, arms and hands**. When resting for some time, the player should **put on a sweat suit** so that the muscles do not get cold, even if it is very hot in the sports hall. The sweat suit should also be worn on the court until the player is really sweating.

Gymnastic bands are very suitable for **stretching exercises**, as they allow **specific muscle groups to be targeted**. Latex bands are marketed as Theraband® or Deuserband®. The latter was developed by Erich Deuser, physical therapist to the German national soccer team in the 1960s, who made the players train with **bicycle tire inner tubes**, among other things. The advantage of the bands is that they allow the player to **choose resistance for the muscles**.

The following exercises are particularly relevant to badminton:

Exercise 1: Hip flexion: Bend the right knee and bring the foot back. Push the foot into the gluteal muscles with the right hand. You should feel a tension in the thigh muscles while you are balancing on one leg. Hold this position for a while, then swap legs and stretch the left leg. If you find it hard to keep your balance, focus your gaze on a particular point in the gym.

Exercise 2: Thigh (back = hamstring): Adopt the lunge position, i.e. take a step forward with one leg until the feet are about a yard apart, making sure that the toes of both feet are pointing forward. The bodyweight should rest on the front, slightly bent leg. The rear leg is straight with the heels on the floor. Now bend the front leg until you feel a definite stretch in the back of the thigh (hamstring). If necessary, increase the distance between your feet in order to increase the amount of stretch. You can place your hands on the front, slightly bent leg for support, keeping your back flat and under no circumstances letting it be hollowed.

Exercise 3: Calf muscles: Adopt the lunge position as in exercise 2, but with your bodyweight over your rear, slightly bent leg. Press the heel to the floor and pull the toe toward the body until you feel a stretch in the calf musculature.

Exercise 4: Calf muscles: Cross your feet so that the left lower leg is crossed in front of the right. Place the feet as close together as possible. Now bend gently forward and try to touch the floor with the palms of your hands if possible. Hold the stretch for a while and then cross the feet the other way around and repeat the exercise.

Exercise 5: Calf muscles: Lean against a wall, supporting yourself with both hands and take the left leg back so that the heel lies flat on the floor. The right leg is placed in front of it and both feet point forward. Slowly shift your bodyweight onto your left leg so that the calf musculature is stretched, then swap leg positions.

Exercise 6: Inner thigh (adductors): Place the feet about shoulder-width apart and the hands on the waist. Then push the hips to the left while twisting the upper body to the right. The right hand slides slowly down the leg. Make sure your body bends to the side, not to the front. Then stretch to the left.

Exercise 7: Shoulders and hips: Place the feet shoulder-width apart. The left hand slides down the trouser seam while the right arm is pulled above the head. It is important that the arm moves above the head and not in front of it, as otherwise the shoulders will not be stretched.

Exercise 8: Shoulder: Stand in front of a wall and move the right arm horizontally backwards. The palm of the hand is placed on the wall while the shoulders are a few inches away from it. Now turn the body to the right to stretch the arm and shoulder, then stretch the other arm and shoulder.

Exercise 9: Wrist: Press the hands together in front of the body with the fingers pointing upward.

Exercise 10: Shoulder and back: Place the right arm behind the head so that the palm of the hand is between the shoulder blades. Place the left arm behind your back and try to touch, or even clasp, your fingertips. After the stretch, swap arm positions.

Exercise 11: Shoulder and chest: Do 10-15 push-ups. This exercise should be performed in training but not in competition as it is very tiring.

Exercise 12: Abs: Sit on the floor with your knees bent and do sit-ups, with your hands behind your head and pull your upper body forward. Try to touch your knees with your right and left elbows alternately.

Exercise 13: Ankle: Balance on one leg without shoes on an uneven surface (e.g. high jump landing mat or sand). Play catch with a soccer ball with a partner to increase the difficulty of the exercise.

Tip 1: Don't make any uncontrolled or sudden movements when warming up. Muscle stretching should be performed with gentle movements and stretches. Stretches should be held for about 10-15 seconds.

Tip 2: The muscles in the human body are arranged so that every muscle has an antagonist, i.e. flexors and extensors. In order to avoid one-sided loading, both muscle groups should be stretched one after the other.

Tip 3: In the individual stretching exercises, the muscles should be stretched in the first phase for about 5-7 seconds, then the stretch should be intensified.

Fig. 119: The Russian Anastasia Russkikh (here in the mixed doubles with the Indonesian Flandy Limpele) has her left leg taped for prophylactic purposes.

19

Fig. 120: European Champion Kenneth Jonassen

19   Technical Jargon

This chapter contains explanations of technical terms. The strokes (clear, smash, drop, drive/flick, short netplay) are not included, as they are described in detail already in previous chapters. As in any other sport, badminton has many special terms that must be understood in order to follow the coach's instructions. Pros already know these terms inside out and sometimes forget that other people are not familiar with them.

Tip: Ask if you don't understand certain terms during a training session. Sometimes the coach may not realize that you don't understand because it is natural for him to use these terms.

Aerobic endurance: exists when a physical performance can be achieved by burning glucose and fatty acids. This process requires the supply of oxygen, so that the endurance level depends on the efficiency of the cardiovascular system. The heart rate lies between 160-170 bpm, which is the individual performance limit and can be improved by aerobic endurance training.

Anaerobic endurance: exists when the body leaves the aerobic area and the energy supplied by burning is no longer sufficient. The body then takes energy from non-oxidative processes, thus creating a lactate deficiency. The heart rate during this form of loading is at least 170 bpm, and untrained athletes quickly suffer from a rapid loss of performance and muscle soreness.

Anticipation: means trying to guess in advance where the opponent will hit the shuttlecock next. The more knowledge one has of motion sequences, speeds and technique, the better one can anticipate the opponent's shots.

Around the head: hitting the shuttlecock to the left of the head. Can be performed for smashes, drops and clears (Chapters 8, 9 and 10).

Back Boundary line: is the back boundary of the court, except in a doubles serve in which case the back boundary line is the long doubles service line which is 30 inches nearer to the net.

Base or Central position: where the player stands in the center of the court, about one step toward the back boundary line in front of the short service line. From this

Fig. 121: Xu Huaiwen lunging.

position, the player can reach all four corners of the court equally well. Players should try to return to this base position after every shot. Ready Position (Chapter 4).

'China' jump: is a running technique (Chapter 14) in which the player jumps to the side with both feet, plays the shot in mid-air and lands with both feet on the ground at the same time. The technique was developed by Chinese players.

Dropshot: refers to a shot played right behind the net, where the opponent's short shot is hit level with the top of the net and drops back into the opponent's court.

Feint: is a surprise or deception shot. The opponent is usually unclear or even deceived about the nature of the stroke until it is actually played. With a sudden movement, the player hits a different stroke to the one that may have been anticipated based on the preceding movement sequence.

Forearm twist: is the rotation of the forearm, which accelerates the stroke, together with the upper arm. The twist is also called the basic turn, and was discovered in sports science analysis. A twist of the right arm to the left produces pronation, and a twist to the right produces supination. Until the mid-1980s, badminton was mistakenly considered to be a sport that was played from the wrist.

Forehand: refers to shots in which the shuttlecock is hit forward with the racket surface i.e. almost with an extension of the palm of the hand. Most forehands are hit at the right of the body, but occasionally also in front or on the left of the body (See Chapter 5).

Formation change: is when doubles players change position during a rally from an attacking formation (one player diagonally in front of the other) to a defensive formation (both players side by side) or vice versa. Tactics (Chapter 15).

Frying pan grip: is a common beginner's mistake. The racket is held so that the player can see the racket surface when he holds it out in front of him. The racket is held like a frying pan or a fly-swatter. The correct grip is obtained by turning the racket through 90°. The frying pan grip is used in exceptional cases by top players to kill or slice the shuttlecock. Grip (Chapter 3).

Half smash: is a shot that is less powerful than a smash. It is used as a variation to the full smash so that after a while the opponent cannot anticipate a full smash.

Kill: is a net play technique in which the shuttlecock is hit above the net very powerfully into the opponent's court. The powerful shot is either produced by a very rapid twist of the forearm or by 'snapping' the wrist.

Kinesio®tape: is a colored bandage for pain or lymph therapy. Some top badminton players have been using the

Fig. 122: Kinesio®tape.

Japanese product for the treatment of tight muscles, strains or torn muscle fibers for some time now. The water and airtight cotton material is coated with a layer of acrylic adhesive and is stuck without being stretched onto the stretched skin.

Lift: is a shot played with a straight arm that is down below the net and can only be reached with a lunge. As with a straight arm it is hard to gain any momentum, the shuttlecock is lifted.

Lunge: is a long step with the right foot towards the shuttlecock. The length of the step means that it is as though one covers two steps in one. Running Technique (Chapter 14).

Neutral position: refers to the starting position before a shot is played. The player is in the ready position and awaits the opponent's shot, then performs the backswing, hits the shuttlecock and follows through. Ready Position (Chapter 4).

Overhand: refers to shots hit above the level of the right shoulder. Hitting Areas (Chapter 5).

Overhead: refers to shots hit above the head. Hitting Areas (Chapter 5).

Plant: the last step with the right foot before playing an overhead shot. The player bends the knees to gain momentum for the upcoming shot by planting the foot almost parallel to the back boundary line. (See Chapters 8 and 10, clear, smash).

Policeman: is a training partner who indicates with his hand or racket in which direction the player should run in shadow badminton training. Running Technique (Chapter 14).

Pre-tensing: means the tensing of muscles before they contract and trigger the actual action. In badminton, the racket must first be brought back before eventually being swing forward with acceleration into the shuttlecock. Pre-tensing makes the action up to 50 % more powerful and explosive than it would be otherwise.

Return: a shot that comes back over the net.

Scissors jump: refers to the running technique (Chapter 14) in which the shuttlecock is hit while running backward. Both feet are off the floor when the shuttlecock is hit, take-off is from the right foot and landing is on the left foot, at which point the body and the right foot are already moving toward the net.

Shadow drill: is an exercise performed without a shuttlecock, where the player runs through positions and/or stroke actions on the court. It enables the player to concentrate fully on the running and stroke techniques.

Shuttle machine: refers to a drill in which the player's partner hits or throws shuttlecocks to the player without returning them. The intensity of the shuttlecock machine drill can be increased by hitting the shuttles very precisely and in very quick succession. Even beginners can confidently perform the role of the "machine".

Sidehand: when the shuttle is hit below shoulder-level and above hip-height. Hitting Areas (Chapter 5).

Slice: the shuttle is "sliced" with a wiping action, and it turns around its transverse axis and spins. It is particularly suitable for dropshots and net play.

Spinning: is a hitting technique at the net in which the racket is held parallel to the net and is pushed like a windscreen wiper into the forehand or backhand area that gives spin to the shuttlecock. This helps the player to avoid touching the net, which would be impossible if he played a 'kill' from this position.

Fig. 123: Overhead shot.

Stab: a hitting technique at net in which the player hits, or 'stabs' the shuttle lighting fast like a fencer at the net, with the surface of the racket almost horizontal to the floor.

Starting step: is an intermediate step with the left foot when moving forward from the ready position. The starting step with the left foot follow a (lunge) step with the right foot. Running Technique (Chapter 14).

Stretching: stretching the musculature before the start of the game. The muscles are warmed up, the joints are mobilized and actions and posture are rehearsed and the concentration is focused on the upcoming match.

T-junction: the area where the center line and short service line meet. About one step behind the t-point toward the back boundary line is the base position. Ready Position (Chapter 4).

Underhand: refers to shots hit below hip-height. This type of shot is a kind of mixture of forehand and backhand.

*Fig. 124: The Chinese player Bao Chunlai
in a state of pre-tension.*

Fig. 125: The umpire keeps an eye on the proceedings.

20 The Rules in Brief

Who hits first?

The toss determines who starts. This can be done the old-fashioned way by tossing a coin, but badminton players usually do it by throwing the shuttlecock up in the air and seeing which way the cork base points when it hits the ground. The winner of the toss has the choice of:

- Serve

- Return of serve

- Side of the court

The toss loser chooses between the remaining options. At the start of the second or third set, the winner of the previous set serves.

Fig. 126: Scoreboard

How does the scoring work?

In the rallypoint scoring system, used worldwide since 2006, the winner is the best of three sets of 21 points. The winner of each rally wins one point to be added to his existing total. Unlike the former scoring system, both the server and returner can win points in each rally.

Can the match be extended?

A set is played over more than 21 points if the score 20 all is reached. The player who then scores two points in a row wins the set. If the score reaches 29 all, the winner of the next point wins the set.

How does the serve work in the singles?

The server starts at 0 and serves all on all even scores from the right service court and hits the shuttlecock into the diagonally opposite side of the opponent's court. On odd-numbered scores he serves from the left.

How does the serve work in the doubles?

The serve follows the same system as the singles, i.e. into the diagonally opposite side of the opponent's court. One of the two doubles partners starts the point with a serve from the right. This player always stands on the right on even point scores, irrespective of whether he is serving or receiving serve. Every time they win a point the partners change sides. If the partners lose the rally, the serve goes to the opponents. The non-serving players rest in their position and receive the service from there.

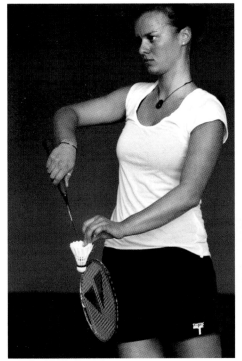

Fig. 127: Correct serve 1

Fig. 128 Correct serve 2

What is the correct serve technique?

- Neither server nor returner should delay the serve once both teams are ready for it; the serve starts once the first backswing has been performed and no interruption is allowed.

- Server and returner must stand in diagonally opposite service courts, with both feet on the floor. Their feet must not touch the lines.

- The server must hit the base of the shuttlecock first.

- The shuttlecock must be hit below waist-height.

- The racket shaft must point in an upwards direction when the shuttlecock is hit.

- The racket must be moved forwards fluently and must not be slowed down or even stopped during the serving action.

- The shuttlecock must fly up over the net and land in the opponent's service court, unless the opponent hits it first.

- The shuttlecock must be hit; not hitting it counts as a foul.

- The server must not serve until the opponent has indicated that he is ready to receive the serve.

- In doubles, the partner can stand wherever he likes as long as he does not obscure the view of the server or returner.

Are there breaks?

A one-minute break is allowed in each set when the first player has scored 11 points, and there is a two-minute break between each set. The basic rule is that after each point, the players should start playing again immediately. Longer breaks between points for recovery or tactical discussions are not allowed, and the players may also not leave the court outside the official break times.

Fig. 129: Even an Olympic Champion is coached at courtside: the Chinese player Lin Dan with his coach.

Can players be coached?

Players can only receive advice when the shuttlecock is not in play and outside the court.

What is a foul?

There is a difference between positional and other fouls. As soon as a foul is spotted, the game must be stopped. A foul usually means that the player who fouled loses possession of the shuttlecock except in the case of positional fouls.

Positional fouls are . . .

*   when a server or receiver has hit out of sequence (in doubles).

*   when the players serve or receive serve from the wrong side of the court.

The positional foul is corrected as soon as it is noticed but the score is unchanged.

Fouls are . . .

*   when the serve is not played correctly (What is the correct serve technique?).

*   if the shuttlecock gets stuck in the net immediately after the serve (it doesn't matter on which side of the net).

*   if the partner of the service receiver returns the serve.

*   if the shuttlecock is not served into the correct part of the court (i.e. diagonally opposite (unless the opponent touches the shuttlecock before it lands).

*   if the shuttlecock touches the floor outside the boundary lines during a point.

*   if the shuttlecock does not clear the net.

*   if the shuttlecock touches the wall or the ceiling (if the ceiling is lower than 10m the serve is repeated if the shuttle touches the ceiling or a ceiling construction.

*   if the shuttlecock touches a player or their clothing.

*   if the shuttlecock is hit by the wood, not the strings.

*   if the shuttlecock is hit by the same player twice in a row (this does not include when it simultaneously touches the racket frame and strings).

*   if the shuttlecock is hit by one player and then by his partner.

*   if a player touches the net with his racket, body or clothing during a rally.

- if a player's body or racket impinge into the opponent's court over the net (underneath the net, the opponent must also be hindered).

- if the opponent is deliberately distracted by actions and gestures.

When is a let played?

A let is played when:

- the serve is hit before the opponent is ready.

- server and receiver both foul at the same time during the serve.

- the shuttlecock touches the net after the serve (irrespective of which side) or gets stuck on the top of the net.

- the cork base becomes detached from the rest of the shuttlecock during a rally.

- (in the umpire's opinion) the game is disturbed or there is a distraction by a spectator.

- an unpredicted or unforeseen event occurs.

Fig. 130: Rikke Olsen from Denmark discusses with the umpire

What is unsporting?

- Delaying or interrupting the game.

- Modifying or damaging the shuttlecock without permission in order to alter the speed or flight properties.

- Verbal or obscene misbehavior directed toward the opponent or the umpire

The umpire signals unsporting behavior with a yellow card (warning) and with a red card if it is repeated (warning) and gross or persistent misbehavior with a black card (warning or disqualification).

What are the court dimensions?

The dimensions can be seen on this diagram. The lines are 4 cm wide and are painted a different color to the rest of the court.

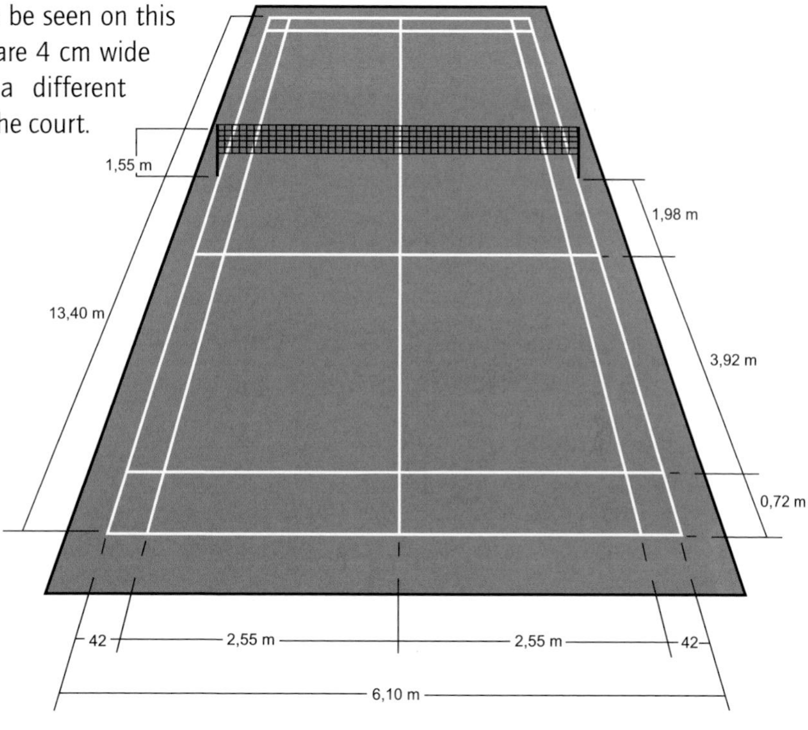

1,55 m

1,98 m

13,40 m

3,92 m

0,72 m

42   2,55 m   2,55 m   42

6,10 m

Fig. 131: The dimensions of the court

What is the shuttlecock made of?

The shuttlecock can be made of natural or synthetic materials and the base (usually made of cork) is usually covered with a thin layer of leather.

- Shuttlecocks have 16 (goose) feathers of the same length (between 62 and 70 mm). The tips of the feathers must form a circle which has a diameter of 58 to 68 mm).

- The feathers must be attached together with a thread and must only weigh between 4.74 and 5.5 grams. The base must have a diameter of 25 to 28 mm.

- Synthetic shuttlecocks should have the same flight properties as natural shuttlecocks.

- A shuttlecock has the correct speed if when it is hit from the back boundary line with a full underarm stroke it lands between 53 and 99 cm from the opponent's back boundary line.

How is the racket constructed?
The overall length and width of the racket frame should not exceed 68 cm and 23 cm respectively, while the stringing should not be longer than 28 cm or wider than 22 cm (there are exceptions for special frame constructions). There is no weight restriction, but apart from the grip, shaft and racket head, the racket should have no other component.

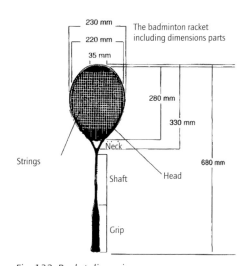

Fig. 132: Racket dimensions

Fig. 133: Young players practicing in the Jaya Raya Club.

21 From the Backyards of Jakarta – Report on Badminton in Indonesia

Badminton is more than just a sport in Indonesia.
It is hot and humid, typical for summer after the rainy season. My shirt sticks to my body, even if I am hardly moving about. In a small sports hall, just a couple of dozen girls aged between 13 and 21 are running around after shuttlecocks. After a while, coach Minarni calls the girls together and assigns them new playing partners. Soon afterwards, the floor of the Rudy Hartono Hall is covered with shuttlecocks. "They train here twice a day," says Minarni, 1968 All England Open doubles champion. The Jaya Raya club is one of over a hundred clubs that are dotted around the Indonesian capital. In the center there are 18, while the rest are found to the north (22 clubs), East (23), South (19) and West (20). Jaya Raya is one of the best training venues for talented youngsters. Even Rudy Hartono (Eight-time All England Champion between 1968 and 1979) trained there. "Not everyone turned pro," says Minarni.

17 Olympic Medals

Fig. 134: The training center for top Indonesian players in Cipayung, South Jakarta

Badminton, or Bulutangkis, as the Indonesians call it, has also always been part of the national consciousness and a source of national pride. No other sport has been so embraced by the South-East Asians as badminton. While other Asian nations, above all China, are also successful in other sports, this is not the case in Indonesia. Although this country with its approximately 15,000 islands and 210 million inhabitants is one of the five most populous countries in the world, until 1992, Indonesians had only won a few Olympic medals. Once badminton was accepted as an Olympic sport, this total changed completely overnight, as Indonesian badminton players have won 17 Olympic medals (including six golds) in the following five games.

The Olympic Games acted as a catalyst in Indonesia. In 1992 the new National Training Center was built in Cipayung and opened by the then Head of State Suharto. The 30 best players live and train there in complete seclusion. The training camp resembles a barracks. On the walls are portraits of the Association Presidents. In the early days of Suharto, military generals were even appointed heads of the association. The extensive facility is situated in Cipayung in South Jakarta and it can only be reached by car. The taxi driver must get out a few times to ask for directions. Narrow lanes in a simple neighborhood. Only just before arriving at our destination do we see a small signpost. At the entrance of the facility, one of the security staff comes out of the sentry box. He is prepared to let me in in exchange for a few Rupiah. The hall has 15 badminton courts.

Badminton is not just an elite sport in Indonesia. In every village and in every neighborhood there is a badminton court. They are in a completely different condition and range from asphalt with painted lines, floodlights, umpire's chair and spectator seating to simple nets with lines laid out made of bamboo sticks.

Games go on until late at night

Fig. 135: 'Bulutangkis' is played until deep into the night on the streets of Jakarta.

"We play every evening, when it is cooler," says 45 year-old Sayfrin. It is dark, and a stranger would never find the backyard court in East Jakarta. And even if he did, he would feel rather queasy. It is a kind of village square surrounded by one-story shacks. The only light comes from the floodlights on the badminton court. There is a lot of talking and children wander around barefoot. Despite the simple way of life, these are not the poorest people out of the capital's millions of residents. Sayfrin says that he works in an office and they consider themselves to be middle class. Sayfrin not only umpires the fixtures/matches for the evening Bulutangkis games, he is also mayor of the Kober/Cakung quarter.

Including floodlights, the neighbors collected around seven million Rupiah (about $ 700) for the badminton court. Sayfrin sweats as he tells me this. He was just standing on the square. We are now sitting in the café that is situated just behind the badminton court. Women bring something to drink and a few men gather around the table. Sayfrin speaks no English and speaks to me through an interpreter. The children who earlier on were running around outside are now squashed around the doorframes in an attempt to overhear what is going on in the house and what the exotic guest says. They would often play at night until 2 or 3am, Sayfrin says. The badminton court is the men's meeting place; there are no women around. While four bare-chested, jeans-clad players are busy on the court playing strokes of varying quality, an umpire keeps an eye on proceedings. He counts the points and jokes from time to time with the men who sit to his left and right on the simple wooden benches. They play with regulation shuttlecocks (or "cocks" as they call them). They even invested up to 400,000 Rupiah in rackets, Sayfrin says.

"Yeah"-Shouting and whistling during international matches

Fig. 136: The "Istora" hall in Jakarta is filled with unruly fans for the Thomas and Uber Cups.

At the Thomas Cup Games involving the Indonesian Team, the "Istora" hall in the center of Jakarta is a sell-out with 10,000 spectators. The atmosphere is like that at a football game. Songs are sung, the crowd does the "Mexican Wave" and the opponents are whistled. The spectators greet the smashes of the Indonesian players with a loud "yeah". They also make a noise by banging inflatable plastic sticks together, instead of the empty shuttlecock tubes that they used to use. June 10th

1967 has gone down in history as the "Day of Shame", when a final of the Thomas Cup against Malaysia was also being played in the "Istora" Hall. The spectators shouted so loudly and behaved so unfairly that the British umpire stopped the match. The Indonesians refused to continue the match in neutral New Zealand and the Malaysians were officially declared winners. "I'm no longer upset that the match was canceled," says 59 year-old Rudy Hartono today. At the time, his glittering career was just beginning; at the time of the infamous match stoppage he was just 17 years old. "The Europeans were not familiar with the atmosphere here, that's why they reacted like that," says Hartono. Today this attitude is also appreciated by the World Badminton Federation. Times have also changed in another respect though, the massive home advantage disappeared in 1994 with the installation of air conditioning. Times in which the hall was completely filled with smoke and players' shirts were already sticking to their backs after one point are now gone forever, but the Indonesians are still enthusiastic when it comes to their national sport.

Fig. 137: Newspapers are full of badminton in Asia.

Fig. 138: In Asia, players like the Malaysian Lee Chong Wei are surrounded by journalists.

22

Fig. 139: Shuttlecock

22 Badminton Glossary

Age Groups, division into playing categories in championships according to age. As well as the General Class (also called "Senior Class"), there are the following categories for young people: under 15, U 17, U 19 and U 22 (juniors), as well as the masters categories of over 35, O 40, O 45, O 50, O 55, O 60, O 65, O 70, O 75. These categories have been changed many times, and until 1998 there were U 16 and U 18 age groups.

Fig. 140: China's Gao Ling won eleven All England titles.

All England, contested since 1899, was considered to be the most prestigious tournament in the world since the introduction of an official *World Championships* in 1977. The All England belongs since the introduction of the *Grand Prix Series* in 1983 to the top tournament league, and since 2007 has been part of the newly introduced *Super Series* since 2007. Until 1993, the

N.B. All terms printed in italics can be looked up in the glossary.

tournament was held in London, and since then in Birmingham. From 1989 to 2006 it offered *prize money* of $ 125,000, and thereafter $ 200,000. In the *Open Era*, *Susi Susanti*, *Morten Frost* and *Lin Dan* are the most successful players, each having won four singles titles. *Ye Zhaoying* and *Xie Xingfang* have each won three titles. In the doubles and mixed doubles, *Gao Ling* has won 11 titles.

Arbi Heryanto, Indonesia, born 1972, was, like his compatriot *Liem Swie King* before him, one of the most spectacular attacking players, specializing in the jump smash. He won the *World Championships* in 1993 and also the *All England* twice, in 1993 and 1994.

Asian Championships, a continental competition that has been contested since 1962. It was not held regularly until 1991 and was also occasionally held as a team competition between the Asian nations. The tournament has been held annually since 1991.

Asian Games, Multi-sport event, first contested in 1951, and since 1954 held every four years. Badminton has been included as a team and individual sport since 1962. Its predecessor was the Far East Games, held since 1913. The most important sports event in Asia after the *Olympic Games*. As well as the Asian Games, there is also the annually contested Asian Badminton Championships, the equivalent of the *European Championships*.

Badminton, name of the estate of the Dukes of Beaufort in the English county of Gloucestershire, called *Badminton House*. The name of the sport is derived from this estate. In some countries the sport has a different name though: Bulutangkis (Indonesia), Pluimbal (South Africa), Sulkapallo (Finland), Tollaslabda (Hungary), Federball (former GDR). Early forms of badminton were called "Poona" (India), "Battledore", "Shuttlecock," "Coquantin" and "Jeu volant" (C17 and C18 Europe).

Badminton Asia Confederation, Governing body of the *Asian National Associations* based in Kuala Lumpur (Malaysia). Was founded on July 30, 1959 and is the oldest continental governing body. Was originally called the Asia Badminton Confederation and was renamed in 2006. The Confederation has 39 member countries and organizes the *Asian Championships*. Official website: *www.badmintonasia.org*.

Badminton Confederation of Africa, Governing Body of 31 *African national associations*. Was founded in 1977 as the African Badminton Confederation and later renamed. The HQ is in Quatre Bornes (Mauritius). The founding nations are Ghana, Mauritius, Mozambique, Kenya, Nigeria and Tansania. Official *website: www.badmintonafrica.org*.

Badminton Europe, Continental Association, founded in 1967 from eleven European associations (including the *German Badminton Association*), first called the European Badminton Union (*EBU*), then renamed Badminton Europe in 2006. It has 51 member associations. Since 1968, it has organized the *European Championships* in the five individual disciplines, since 1972 the team European Championships. Since 1968 the Youth European Championships (since 1975 the team European Championships. The BE circuit was introduced in 1988 with international championships in Europe (prize money below the *Grand Prix Series*). Since 1978 annual contesting of the Europe Clubs Championships. Since 1995, *European Senior Championships* (O 35 to O 65). Official website: *www.badmintoneurope.com*.

Fig. 141: Badminton Gazette

Badminton Gazette, was the official newsletter of the *Badminton Association of England*. The newsletter was founded in 1907 and ran for 72 years until 1979.

Editors included such sporting celebrities as *George Thomas* (1907-12, 1913-15), *Herbert Scheele* (1946-1977) and Pat Davis (1970-79). The Badminton Gazette was also for a long time the only international publication. "World Badminton" published by the *BWF*, was launched in 1972, and existed until 1996. Since the end of the 90s, information about international events has been available on internet.

Fig. 142: Badminton House

Badminton House, seat of the Somerset family inhabited by the Duke of Beaufort. Badminton was invented in the great hall of the English estate in 1850. Older games with a shuttlecock are also known in Asia and South America. The first rules were published by an unknown author in England as the "Rules for the New Games of Tennis and Badminton."

Badminton Oceania, continental governing body, was founded in 1987 as Oceania Badminton Confederation. The Association now has nine member countries and its headquarters is in Victoria (Australia). Official website: www.oceaniabadminton.org.

Badminton Pan Am, continental governing body, founded in 1976. The association has 30 member countries and is headquartered in Lima, Peru. It was originally called the Pan American Badminton Confederation. Official website: www.badmintonpanam.org.

Badminton World Federation (BWF), international governing body, founded in London in 1934 by the Associations of England, Ireland, Scotland, Wales, Denmark, France, the Netherlands, New Zealand and Canada. It was called the International Badminton Federation (IBF) until 2006. The *BWF* has 159 members states throughout the five continental confederations: Europe (51), Asia (39), Africa (32), Americas (30), Oceania (8). The *BWF* HQ is in Kuala Lumpur (Malaysia) and is governed by a President, elected Council and Annual General Members' meeting. Between 1979 and 1981, a short-lived rival world federation, the World Badminton Federation (WBF) also existed, which was founded because of the China-Taiwan issue. The *BWF* organizes the *World Championships*, *Thomas and Uber Cup*, *Sudirman Cup* and the *Super Series*. Official website: www.internationalbadminton.org.

Bang Soo-Hyun, Korea, born in 1972, was the great rival of the legendary Indonesian *Susi Susanti* and often had to settle for second place. Her career highlights were Gold in the 1996 *Olympics* and *All England Championships*. With Korea she won the *Sudirman Cup* twice, in 1991 and 1993. She was elected to the BWF Council (2005-2009).

Beachminton, beach version of badminton, presented by the inventors at the ISPO in Munich in 1998. The 3.8 x 12.3 meter court is smaller than the badminton court. The lines are marked with fabric or rubber bands in the sand. The shuttle is heavier than a badminton shuttle and the net is slightly higher. Beachminton can be played both indoors and outdoors.

Fig. 143: Eddy Choong

Choong, Eddy, Malaysia, *Hall of Fame* member, born in 1930. In the 1950s he dominated the international scene with his brother David and introduced the Asian dominance of the sport that continues to this day. He was eight-time winner of the *All England* (1951-57), four times in the singles. He won six *German Open* titles (1955-57) in men's singles, men's doubles and mixed doubles.

Commonwealth Games, a multi-sports event contested every four years by all the nations who recognize the British Queen as their Head of State since 1930. Badminton has been included since

1966 and is dominated by England and Malaysia.

Day of Shame, the stopping of the *Thomas Cup* finals on June 10th 1967 was a black day in the history of the sport. The Indonesian hosts were playing against the challengers Malaysia in front of 12,000 spectators in the Senayan stadium in Jakarta. With the score at 3:3, the umpire *Herbert Scheele* wanted the game to continue in camera because of biased spectators. As the Indonesians refused this, and also a rematch in neutral New Zealand, Malaysia was officially declared winner with a score of 6:3.

Doping, illegal performance enhancement, which makes little sense in badminton according to expert information, due to the complexity of the sport. Constant testing in training and at national and international competitions. In 1998 there was the then unique spectacular doping case of the Indonesian *Budiarto Sigit*, who was found guilty of taking the anabolic steroid Nandrolone. The *BWF* banned him for two years.

Equal Rights, essential element in Badminton, one of few sports in which men and women compete together in teams. All five disciplines (men's and women's singles, men's and women's doubles and mixed doubles) are always contested in tournaments. The *BWF* prevented a separation into men's and women's tournaments after 1992, after the IOC initially banned the mixed doubles (as in tennis and table tennis) from the *Olympic* program and only reinstated it in 1996. Since 2008, women and men have received the same *prize money* in international competitions.

European Championships, first held in 1968, contested in individual and team disciplines. Takes place every year from 2010, before that it was every two years. Since 1969, youth age groups have also been included. It is organized by *Badminton Europe*. Dominated by Danish and English players. Championships are also contested in the other four *continental federations*.

144: Morten Frost

Frost Morten, Denmark, born in 1958, *Hall of Fame* member. He dominated the scene in the 1980s, reached the *All England* men's singles finals eight times in a row and won four times (1982, 84, 86 and 87), European Champion in 1984 and 1986. Lost the World Championships final twice in 1985 and 1987 losing dramatically the first time to *Han Jian* after leading until the side change in the 3rd set by 8:3, and then failing to win a single serve. The first

badminton millionaire, he later worked as a coach in Denmark, Malaysia and South Africa.

Fig. 145: Peter Gade

Gade Peter, Denmark, born in 1976, topped the World Rankings from 1998 to 2001. European men's singles champion in 1998, 2000, 2004 and 2006 and All England champion in 1999. He often failed in big tournaments due to his nervous temperament, e.g. losing a match point in the semi-finals of the men's singles in the home World Championships in 1999. Reached the World Championships final in 2001 and won 16 *Grand Prix Series* titles. Formerly engaged to *Camilla Martin*.

Gao Ling, China, born 1979, *Hall of Fame* member, winner of four Olympic medals and four *World Championships* titles, the most successful female player of all time. She won Olympic gold in the mixed doubles in 2000 and 2004 and silver (2004) and bronze (2000) in the women's doubles. She won the *World Championships* ladies doubles three times

(2001, 2003 and 2006) and the mixed doubles once (2001), as well as eleven *All England* titles.

Gilks, Gillian, England, born in 1950, *Hall of Fame* member, in 1976, she was first female player to win the *All England* in women's singles, women's doubles and mixed doubles, won 23 titles in the *Grand Prix Series*, even though this was only first contested in 1983, when Gillian was already 33 years old. She was World Championship women's singles runner-up in 1977. Her approximately 600 victories make her one of the most successful title collectors of all time. In the European Championships alone she won a world record 12 titles. A biography about her called "A Life of Badminton" was published in 1981.

Gong Ruina, China, born in 1981, was the first female player after winning the World Junior Championships (1998) to also win the *World Championships* (2001). She won the *All England* in 2004 as well as 5 other *Grand Prix tournaments*. In the 2004 *Olympics*, she lost the bronze medal play-off against her countrywoman Zhou Mi and ended her career shortly afterwards at the age of 25. Won the Uber Cup with China in 2002 and 2004.

Gong, Zhichao, China, born in 1977, won gold in the 2000 *Olympics*, beating the Dane *Camilla Martin* in the final. She won two *All England* singles titles in 2000 and 2001. Won the Uber Cup twice with China in 1998 and 2000.

Grand Prix Final, an end of season tournament contested from 1983 to 2000 by the best players in the *Grand Prix rankings* and later the *World Rankings* played off at the end of the season. The highest prize money ($ 380,000) was offered there in 1997. Since 2008 there is the Super Series Final at the end of the year. The *prize money* is $ 500,000. The best players of the Super-Series-Ranking in each discipline are allowed to participate.

Grand Prix Rankings, ranking list of the best players in the *Grand Prix Series*, published from 1983 to 1996 by the *BWF*. At the end of the season, the best players in each discipline qualified for the *Grand Prix Final*. The best 25 players/pairings received a prize out of a bonus pool. With the introduction of the *World Rankings* in 1990, the additional Grand Prix rankings led to confusion and were discontinued.

Grand Prix Series, a tournament series that was started in 1983. The *BWF* brought together the international championships offering more than a certain minimum prize money. The series included between 7 and 20 tournaments. The average prize money per tournament rose from just $ 28,000 in 1984 to $ 150,000 in 2006. The *All England*, the Japan Open, the Indonesia Open and the Malaysia Open were always included. The *German Open* joined in 1984. In 2007, the *Super Series* superseded the *Grand Prix Series* as the elite series, the *Grand Prix Series* still exists but is now a 2nd tier tournament.

The best players from the Grand Prix Series qualified for the *Grand Prix Final*. As well as prize money, players also win *world ranking* points according to their class and performance.

Gunawan, Tony, Indonesia, born in 1975, won 35 international men's and mixed doubles titles with a variety of partners. With Candra Wijaya, he won *Olympic* gold in 2000 and won the *World Championships* with Halim Haryanto in 2001 and with Howard Bach (USA) in 2005. Gunawan emigrated from Indonesia to the USA in 2002 and also competed in tournaments for his new homeland.

Fig. 146: Punch Gunalan

Gunulan, Punch, Malaysia, born in 1944, player, coach and *BWF* official, . Won the *All England* men's doubles in 1971 and reached the men's singles final in 1974, won the *Asian Games* in men's singles and doubles in 1970. Later became a coach and manager in Malaysia, from 1997 was Vice President of the *BWF* and from 2005 to 2008, was General

Secretary of the Federation, moved the Headquarters to Kuala Lumpur and worked on the *internationalization* of the sport. Became embroiled in an internal power struggle with BWF President Kang Young-Joong (Korea) and retired in 2008.

Hadinata, Christian, Indonesia, born in 1949 *Hall of Fame* member, had a brilliant record in the *Thomas Cup* where he won only lost one event between 1973 and 1986 and won the title four times with Indonesia (1973, '76, '79 and '84). Hadinata started out as a singles player (*All England* finalist in 1973) his career highlight being the 1980 *World Championships* where he won the men's and mixed doubles. He is now coach for doubles of the Indonesian national team.

Hall of Fame, badminton roll of honor founded in 1996 on the initiative of BWF Vice-President Roy Ward (Australia), the founding members were Colonel S S C Dolby, *Sir George Thomas*, *Betty Uber* and *Herbert Scheele*. The hall of fame now contains 51 names of players and officials. The roll of honor can be seen in Kuala Lumpur (Malaysia) at the *BWF* Headquarters.

Han Aiping, China, born in 1962, was the first player to defend a *World Championships* title in ladies singles (1985 and 1987), also won the *World Championships* in ladies doubles in 1985. The first world class female Chinese player after China joined the *BWF* in 1981, dominated the 1980s with Li Lingwei.

Han Jian, China, born in 1956, *Hall of Fame* member, won the men's singles *World Championships* in 1985 against *Morten Frost* at the age of 29. He was the matchwinner in the *Thomas Cup* victory in 1982 just after China had joined the *BWF* the previous year. He beat the legendary Indonesian *Liem Swie King* 17:14 in the third set.

Fig. 147: Rudy Hartono

Hartono Rudy, Indonesia, born in 1949, *Hall of Fame* member, record-holder with eight titles in the men's singles in the *All England* (1968-78). Men's singles world champion in 1980, *Thomas Cup* (1970, 73, 76 and 79). Later became a businessman (badminton equipment) and *BWF* official.

Hashman, Judy, America, born 1936 née Delvin. *Hall of Fame* member at 18 years of age won the first of ten *All England* ladies singles titles (1954, 57, 58, 60-64, 66, 67) as well as seven ladies doubles titles. Her father Frank Devlin (Ireland) won the *All England* 18 times. Hashman lost only once in the *Uber Cup* in

14 years, winning three titles with the USA (1957, 60 and 63).

Fig. 148: Taufik Hidayat

Hidayat, Taufik, Indonesia, born 1981, was the first player to win the men's singles in both the *Olympic Games* (2000) and the *World Championships* (2005). Is considered something of a bad seed, after being fined $ 2,500 by the *BWF* in 2006 for leaving the court in protest at a line judge's decision. A biography about him was published in Indonesia in 2003. Winner of the *Thomas Cup* (2000 and 2002).

Høyer-Larsen, Poul-Erik, Denmark, born in 1965, was the first non-Asian winner (at the age of 30) of an Olympic Gold medal in 1996. Two-time winner of the *All England* singles in 1995 and 1996 and three-time European Champion in 1992, '94 and '96.

International Badminton Federation (IBF), original name of the *Badminton World Federation*

International Matches, interface between two countries. Friendly matches as well as matches at the *World Championships, European Championship, Sudirman Cup* and Thomas and *Uber Cups*. The first international match in badminton history took place on January 31st 1903 between Ireland and England (2:5), and the two countries played each other once a year until 1972. The first international match in the *Thomas Cup* was played on November 2nd 1948 between Denmark and Ireland (9:0) in Copenhagen in the first round of the Europe zone. The first women's international match in the *Uber Cup* was contested by Hong Kong and Malaysia (1:6) on August 30th 1957.

Internationalization, attempt by the *World Federation* to popularize and professionalize the sport of badminton. The *BWF* has managed international training centers in Saarbrücken (Germany), Sofia (Bulgaria) and Guangzhou (China) since 2005, where particularly players from countries hitherto underrepresented in tournaments can improve their game. This enabled players from 50 countries to qualify for the 2008 *Olympics* in Beijing. The World Federation also provides international training for coaches and in 2004 increased the number of countries participating in the *Thomas and Uber Cups* from eight to twelve.

Ji, Xingpeng, born in 1977. Surprise *Olympic* gold medal winner in 2000, as his countryman *Xia Xuanze* was actually more strongly favored to win. The 22 year

Fig. 149: Ji Xingpeng

old had also won the Japan Open in the same year, but both victories were the only ones of his career, which ended soon afterwards. He went on to work as a coach in the national training camp in Beijing.

Fig. 150: Kim Dong-Moon

Kim, Dong-Moon, Korea, born in 1975, *Hall of Fame* member, is the only player to win *Olympic* gold in both the Men's doubles (2004) and Mixed doubles (1996), and *World Championships* gold in Men's doubles (1999) and Mixed doubles in 1999 and 2003. With Ra

Kyung-Min (whom he went on to marry in 2005), he won four *All England* titles (1998, 2000, 2002 and 2004) and in 2003 won ten *Grand Prix* tournaments in a row, they were unbeaten for 70 games.

Kobberø, Finn, Denmark, 1936-2009, *Hall of Fame* member, was a world-class player in all three disciplines in the 50s and 60s. At the *All England*, he won 7 times in Men's doubles and 8 times in Mixed doubles and reached the Men's singles finals 3 times. In the *Thomas Cup*, he won 55 of his 64 matches, and reached the finals twice with Denmark in 1955 and 1964. He also won 22 national Danish titles.

Fig. 151: Lene Køppen

Køppen, Lene, Denmark, born 1953, *Hall of Fame* member was the first European female player to become women's doubles world champion in 1977, and the Danish postal service celebrated her success in the 1983 home *World Championships* by issuing a 2.70 Dk stamp. Two-time winner of the *All England* women's singles in 1979 and 1980.

Kops, Erland, Denmark, born 1937, *Hall of Fame* member, ended England's dominance in Europe at the end of the 1950s. Won 11 *All England* titles, 7 of which in men's singles (1958, '60, '61, '62, '63, '65 and '67) and 4 in men's doubles (1958, '67, '68 and '69). With Denmark lost the *Thomas Cup* final in 1964 against Indonesia (4:5).

Kusuma, Alan Budi, Indonesia, born 1968, first Gold medal winner at the *Olympic Games* in 1992. Formed a dream pairing with *Susi Susanti*. He also won eight tournaments in the *Grand Prix series*. Won the *World Cup* in 1993 and the *Thomas Cup* in 1996. He lost the 1991 *World Championships* final against *Zhao Jianhua*.

Fig. 152: Li Lingwei

Li, Lingwei, China, born in 1964, *Hall of Fame* member. Belonged to the first generation of Chinese players who caused a sensation when China joined the *BWF* in 1981. Won the women's singles *World Championships* in 1983 and 1989, and the women's doubles in 1985. Dominated the scene in the 1980s with *Han Aiping*. Uber Cup winner in 1984, 1986 and 1988. She won 21 women's *Grand Prix tournaments* in women's singles, was two-time *All England* women's singles champion in 1984 and 1989 and went on to become a coach and official.

Fig. 153: Li Yongbo

Li, Yongbo, China, born in 1962, with Tian Bingyi formed one of the strongest doubles pairings in the world in the mid-80s. Their great rivals were the Koreans *Park Joo-Bong* and Kim Moon-Soo. He won the *World Championships* men's doubles twice in 1987 and 1989, the *All England* in 1987, '88 and '91 and the *Thomas Cup* in 1986, '88 and '90). In 1992, he won the bronze medal in the 1992 *Olympic Games*. He is now head coach of the Chinese national team.

Liem Swie King, Indonesia, born in 1956, *Hall of Fame* member, famous for his high jump smash. He reached the *All England* men's singles final from 1976 to 1981, winning three times (1978, '79 and '81). His finals defeat in the 1985

World Championships at the hands of countryman Icuk Sugiarto is legendary, when he lost 16:17 in the third set after one hour and 40 minutes. In 2009 a film of the life of Liem Swie King was produced in Indonesia.

Fig. 154: Lin Dan

Lin, Dan, China, born in 1983. The most successful player of all time. Gold medallist in the *Olympic Games* in 2008 and two-time world champion (2006, '07). *All England* champion in 2004, 2006 and 2007 and winner of 19 more international tournaments including the *Thomas Cup* in 2006 and 2008, the *Sudirman Cup* in 2005 and 2007. It engaged to two-time Chinese women's world champion *Xie Xingfang*.

Lu, Shengrong, China, born in 1940, *Hall of Fame* member, President of the *BWF* from 1993 to 2001, from 1996 to 2001, was the second representative of the sport of badminton at the IOC along with Craig Reedie (England). Lu was the first woman to head an international sports federation and was particularly active in promoting women's issues in the sport.

Fig. 155: Thomas Lund

Lund, Thomas, Denmark, born in 1968, *Hall of Fame* member. Specialist in men's and mixed doubles and record *Grand Prix series* winner with 51 titles. Two-time world mixed doubles champion in 1993 and 1995, as well as winner of 9 *All England* titles, 6 in men's doubles and 3 in mixed doubles. Won 5 successive *Grand Prix finals* from 1990 to 1994. Was sports director of the Danish Badminton Federation and has been COO of the *BWF* in Kuala Lumpur since 2009.

Fig. 156: Camilla Martin

Martin, Camilla, Denmark, born 1974. In 1999, was the second European women's singles world champion after *Lene*

Køppen. Olympic silver medallist in 2000, three-time European champion (1996-2000). *All England* champion in 2002. Was engaged to *Peter Gade*. Her father was a goalkeeper for Glasgow Rangers.

National Associations, organizations responsible for the organization of the sport of badminton in different countries. England was the first country to found a national association on September 12th in Southsea, 1893, and 14 clubs were present at the inauguration of the Badminton Association of England (BA of E). The first President was Colonel S.S.C. Dolby, also a *Hall of Fame* member

Fig. 157: Ticket for the preliminary badminton rounds in Barcelona 1992.

Olympic Games Badminton has been on the Olympic program since 1992, initially without the mixed doubles, which was included in 1996. Badminton was a demonstration sport for one day in Munich in 1972, and in 1988 at the request of the South Korean hosts. Since then, all gold medals have gone to Asian players, with the exception of *Poul-Erik Høyer-Larsen* in 1996. The *BWF* reformed under pressure from the IOC with regard to television rights, and the changed *scoring system* and *internationalization* also date from this time.

Open Era, professional era of prize money tournaments, introduced in 1979 by the *BWF*. The term 'open' in tournament names means they are open to both professionals and amateurs. As the IOC adhered to/retained amateur status until the start of the 80s, many players reacted cautiously to the new opportunities to win money in prize money tournaments. With the introduction of the *Grand Prix Series* in 1983, the *professionalization* and the abolition of the amateur status at the IOC could no longer be stopped. *Prize money* is constantly increasing in the top events.

Fig. 158: Park Joo-Bong

Park, Joo-Bong, Korea, born in 1964, *Hall of Fame* member, and best men's and mixed doubles player in the world from the mid 80s to the mid 90s. He won Olympic gold in the mixed doubles in 1996 and silver in the mixed doubles in 1996. He was world men's doubles champion in 1985 and 1991 and mixed doubles champion in 1985, '89 and '91, and *Sudirman Cup* winner in 1991 and 1993. After *Thomas Lund*, he is the most successful player with 47 titles in the

Grand Prix Series and 9 *All England* titles. He went on to work as a coach in England, Malaysia and Japan.

Pri, Svend, Denmark, born in 1983, was eight-time Danish champion between 1966 and 1975, and was the successor to countryman *Erland Kops*. His victory in the 1975 *All England* ended the winning streak of the Indonesian *Rudy Hartono*, who had gained 7 successive victories.

Prize Money, sums of money distributed according to an allocation system in international tournaments, usually paid in US Dollars. The first tournament in the *Open Era* was the Friends Provident Masters invitation tournament in London in September 1979. The winners, *Lene Køppen* and Prakash Padukone had to pay their prize money to their national associations, as they were not yet registered as professionals. A total of three million USD was given out in the 2006 *Grand Prix Series*. The highest *prize money* ever given in a badminton tournament was the $ 500,000 offered in the 2008 *Super Series Final*.

Professionalization, conditions that enable the player to concentrate fully on his sport. Professionalization in badminton was particularly due to the *Open Era* and the earning opportunity offered by *prize money* and sponsors. The first licensed professional player was Joanna Flockhart (Scotland) in 1979. The *BWF* promoted the professional *internationalization* of the sport with training centers and coach's education.

Rallypoint, scoring system introduced by the World Federation in 2006. Since then, in all competitions through the world, in all 5 disciplines the winner is the best of three sets up to 21 points. The winner of every rally gains a point, and an advantage of at least 2 points is necessary to win a set, until 29 all, in which case the winner of the next point wins the match. The games are an average of 30 % shorter than under the old scoring system.

Fig. 160: Betty and Herbert Scheele

Scheele, Herbert, England, 1905-1981, *Hall of Fame* member, legendary official, his most important post being Secretary of the *BWF* from 1938 to 1976. He also performed this duty for the English Badminton Association from 1945-1970. He managed the affairs from his residence in Kent and was actively supported by his wife Betty (1914-2009). He was an international umpire from 1938-1976, and stopped the *Thomas Cup* final on the *Day of Shame* in 1967. From 1946-1970, he was editor of the *Badminton Gazette*. He was awarded the Order of the British Empire (OBE) by the Queen. The Herbert Scheele trophy was named after him, with which the Board of the *BWF* has honored personalities for outstanding service since 1986. The 14 recipients have included *Rudy Hartono* (1986), *Erland Kops* (1989), *Eddy Chong* (1994) and *Susi Susanti* (2002).

Fig. 159: Peter Rasmussen

Rasmussen, Peter, Denmark, born in 1974, the only European player to win the *World Championships* (1997) and European Championships (2002) men's singles. Rasmussen always missed qualification for the *Olympic Games*. His 1997 World Championships final against Sun Jun (China) is a classic. It lasted two hours (198 ball exchanges) and Sun suffered from cramps at the end of the third set but played until the end.

Scoring system, rule for counting points. For almost 100 years, badminton had used an unaltered system (the best of three sets up to 15 points, only the server could score, at 13 all, the game could go to 18 points, and at 14 all to 17 points). An exception have been Ladies singles, which were best of three sets up to 11 points. In 1995, Norway tested the system of playing the best of 5 sets to 9 points for 1 year. In 2001, the *BWF* introduced the best of 5 sets to 7 points. Since 2006, the international scoring system has been the 3 x 21 *rally point* scoring system.

Shuttlecocks, also shuttle, bird, birdie, consist of 16 feathers weighing between 4.7 and 5.2 grams. The feathers must all have the same length, between 62 and 70 mm (2.3-2.7 inches). The pointed ends of the feathers form a circle with a diameter of 58 to 68 millimeters (~2.3-2.7 inches), and the feathers themselves are stuck in a cork base. Beginners also use synthetic shuttlecocks with comparable flight quality.

Sidek brothers, Malaysian badminton family, all world class players, Misbun (born 1960), Razif (born 1962), Jalani (born 1963), Rahman (born 1965) and Rashid (born 1968). Their greatest success was in the *Thomas Cup* in 1992, in which Razif and Jalani took part in the doubles and Rashid in the singles. Sister Zamaliah also participated in a *World Championships*. The Sidek brothers invented the so-called Sidek serve in which the shuttle feathers are hit first so that the shuttlecock trickles over the net

to the opponent. This serve was later banned.

Fig. 161: Budiarto Sigit

Sigit, Budiarto, Indonesia, born in 1975, responsible for badminton's first spectacular *doping* case. Sigit was found guilty of taking the anabolic steroid Nandrolone. The *BWF* banned the 1997 world men's doubles champion from all national and international tournaments for one year. Sigit's doubles partner Chandra Wijaya later won gold at the Sydney *Olympic Games* in 2000 with replacement Tony Gunawan.

Speed, badminton is one of the fastest sports in the world. A smash played by the Chinese doubles player Fu Haifeng during the *Sudirman Cup* in 2005 was measured at 332 km/h (206.3 mph). For comparison purposes: in squash the world record is 270 km/h (168 mph) by John White, the tennis world record (249.4 km/h or 155 mph) by Andy Roddick. Only golf tee shots at around

300 km/h (186.5 mph) can approach speeds achieved in badminton.

Fig. 162: Postage stamp featuring Lin Dan

Stamps, Indonesia is the most prolific issuer of badminton stamps in the world. In 1958, during the first *Thomas Cup* victory, the first series of three stamps was produced. Japan, China, Denmark and Sweden followed suit. Since badminton has been an Olympic sport, Spain, Grenada, Macau, Hungary, Mauritius and Surinam have all issued badminton stamps.

Sudirman Cup, Team World Championships for mixed teams, held every two years since 1989. Until 2001, the Sudirman Cup took place in connection with the Individual World Championships and at the same venue. The Cup is named for the former Indonesian Association president Dick Sudirman. Three countries dominate the list of winners: China (6 times), Korea (3 times), Indonesia (once). One game per international match is played in the men's singles, women's singles, men's doubles, women's doubles and mixed doubles.

Sugiarto, Icuk, Indonesia, born in 1962, in a memorable *World Championships*

final in 1983, he beat his countryman and favorite *Liem Swie King* 17:16 in the 3rd set after 90 minutes after defending 3 match points. Two-time winner of the World Cup in 1985 and 1986 and 9 *Grand Prix tournaments*. Was on the winning *Thomas Cup* team in 1984.

Sun, Jun, Chinese, born 1975, won the *World Championships* in 1999 after losing 2 years previously in a legendary final against *Peter Rasmussen* because of a cramp but he still played the match until the end. He was feared for his spectacular showmanship on court. He won the *All England* in 1988, the *World Cup* in 1997 and the Grand Prix final in 1997 and '98, and the *Sudirman Cup* twice with China in 1995 and 1999. He also won 3 other *Grand Prix tournaments*. He was the 1st player to become senior world champion after also winning the World Junior Championships in 1992.

Super Series, tournament series introduced in 2007. The Super Series replaced the *Grand Prix series* that had existed since 1983 as the top event in the *BWF* calendar. The tournament organizers must offer *prize money* of at least $ 200,000. The series includes 4 European tournaments (England, Denmark, Switzerland and France), and 8 in Asia. Only the best players in the *world rankings* are eligible to play and players must also go through qualification rounds in order to reach the main draw. At the end of each year the *Super Series Final* takes place with the best players in each discipline. They are taken from the Super-Series-Ranking.

Fig. 163: Susi Susanti

Susanti, Susi, Indonesia, born in 1971. *Hall of Fame* member, she dominated the women's singles between 1989 and 1997. The delicate woman (5'3", 115 pounds) could do the splits when lunging to reach the shuttlecock. Her women's singles successes: in the *Olympic Games* gold medal in 1992, bronze medal in 1996, in the *World Championships* 1993, in the *Uber Cup* 1994 and '96, in the *Sudirman Cup* 1989, in the *World Cup* in 1989, '93, '94, '96 and '97, in the *Grand Prix final* from 1990-'94 and 1996, 33 *Grand Prix tournaments* (including 4 *All England* titles). Married to Alan Budi Kusuma (Gold in the 1992 *Olympic Games* men's singles).

Thomas Cup, Men's team World Championships, first contested in 1949, until 1982 every 3 years and since then every 2 years. The cup is named after the founder *Sir George Thomas*. Until now, 3 countries have dominated the winner's list: Indonesia (13 times), China (7 times) and Malaysia (5 times). Each

international match includes two men's doubles and three men's singles games. Since 1984, the final round has been played together with the *Uber Cup*. The title defender, the host, 4 teams from Asia, 3 from Europe and 1 each from Africa, Americas and Oceania participate in the final round.

Fig. 164: Sir George Thomas

Thomas, Sir George Alan, England, 1881-1972. *Hall of Fame* member. Pioneer of the sport of badminton. Inaugural President of the *BWF* until 1995. Wrote the book "The Art of Badminton" (1925). Thomas started a team World Championships back in 1939, but due to WW2, the eponymous *Thomas Cup* was first contested only in 1949. He won 21 *All England* titles and was also a successful tennis player (quarter finals at Wimbledon in 1920 and 23) and British chess champion.

Fig. 165: Betty Uber

Fig. 166: Umpire

Uber, Betty, England, née Corbin, 1906-1983, *Hall of Fame* member, won 13 *All England* titles between 1930 and 1949. She founded the women's team World Cup, the *Uber Cup*, in 1956. She was a Junior Wimbledon tennis champion and wrote the book: "That Badminton Racket."

Uber Cup, women's team World Championships, first contested in 1957, every 3 years until 1984, and every 2 years since then. The cup is named after its founder *Betty Uber*. Four countries have dominated the winner's list until now: China (11 times), Japan (5 times), USA and Indonesia (3 times each). Each international match includes two women's doubles and three women's singles games. Since 1984, the Uber Cup has been held in conjunction with the *Thomas Cup*.

Umpire, enforces the rules of the game during a match. In important tournaments there is also a service umpire and up to 10 line judges.

World Badminton Federation (WBF) an alternative to the *International Badminton Federation* founded in Hong Kong in 1979 whose members are 13 Asian and 6 African nations. There are 4 reasons for the split of the World Federations: 1) the *IBF* proposal to exclude Taiwan in order to accept China. 2) the desire to give every member nation a voice. 3) the lack of understanding that England, Wales, Scotland and Ireland each count as one country. 4) That South Africa could be in the *IBF* despite its apartheid regime. On 26 May 1981, the *IBF* and WBF united to form one Federation and China joined the Federation.

World Championships, individual and team tournament, have been contested at senior level since 1977, initially every three years (1977-'83) then every two years (1985-'05) and since then annually (with the exception of Olympic years). They are organized by the *BWF*. From 1989 to 2001, the team World Championships (*Sudirman Cup*) is held in the week before the individual World Championships at the same venue. The World Junior Championships (U 19) has existed since 1992. There is also the prestigious team World Championships for men, the *Thomas Cup* and for women (*Uber Cup*).

World Cup, *WBF* invitation tournament from 1981 to 1997 and 2005 and 2006. The World Cup has always been one of the most prestigious tournaments and paved the way for badminton to become a *professional sport*. Even in 1981, the *prize money* offered was $118,000.

World Rankings, introduced in 1990 by the World Federation, initially sued to determine the participants in the *Olympic Games*. Players and pairings received points for the ranking lists according to their performance in tournaments. The number of points is determined by the grade of the tournament (1-7 stars). The world ranking list includes the 10 best tournament results for the previous 12 months. The *BWF* publishes the new ranking list every Thursday on its website, it is used both for Olympic qualification and admission to certain tournaments. From 1983 to 1996, the *BWF* ran a *Grand Prix ranking list* which started again from zero every season.

World Training Centers, training venues for talented players from different nations inaugurated by the *BWF* in 2005. They are located in Saarbrücken (Germany), Guangzhou (China) and Sofia (Bulgaria). They offer players high-level training courses of different lengths which they would not otherwise have in their home countries. They were intended to contribute to the *internationalization* of the sport.

Fig. 167: Xia Xuanze

Xia, Xuanze, Chinese, born in 1979, won the *World Championships* in 2003, bronze medal in the 2000 *Olympic Games*, member of the winning *Thomas Cup* team in 2004.

Xie, Xingfang, Chinese born in 1981, winner of the women's singles *World Championships* in 2005 and 2006, silver medal in the *Olympic Games* in 2008.

Fig. 168: Xie Xingfang

Three *All England* women's singles titles (2005-'07). Engaged to *Lin Dan*. Has adorned the front page of several Chinese magazines.

Fig. 169: Xu Huaiwen

Xu, Huaiwen, born in 1975, born in Chengdu, China. Has held German nationality since 2003. She won the

European Championships women's singles twice in 2006 and 2008, five times national women's champion (2004-'08), 52 *international matches* for Germany. Participated in the 2004 *Olympic Games* (lost in the 1st round), and 2008 (lost in the quarter finals). Was the first German player to win a *Grand Prix Series* tournament in women's singles (Helexpo Thessaloniki 2005). She retired in 2009.

Yang, Yang, Chinese, born 1963, was the first player to defend his *World Championship* singles title ('87 and '89), won the *Thomas Cup* 3 times with China ('86, '88, and '90). He won 12 big international championships, including the *Grand Prix final* in 1986, the *World Cup* in 1988 and 1990 and the *All England Open* in 1989. He also won the demonstration event at the *Olympic Games* in 1988. In 1991 he retired and became a coach in Malaysia, winning the *Thomas Cup* with that country in 1992. He founded a badminton equipment firm, returned to China in 2000 and founded an eponymous badminton club in Nanjing.

Yuki, Hiroe, Japanese, born in 1950. *Hall of Fame* member, the most successful Japanese player ever, won the *Uber Cup* three times with her country in 1969, '72 and '78. Won the *All England* 4 times in women's singles (1969, '74, '75 and '77).

Zhang, Ning, Chinese, born in 1975, in 2008, was the first woman to defend the

Fig. 170: Zhang Ning

admitted that Zhang Ning's victory over countrywoman Zhou Mi in the 2004 semi-finals was fixed. She retired in 2008 and now is national coach.

Zhao, Jianhua, Chinese, born in 1965, won the *All England* at his first attempt in 1985 in a final against *Morten Frost*, and also won in 1990. Won the *World Championships* in 1991, the *Grand Prix final* in 1991 and the *World Cup* in 1987. Lost the *Olympic Games* in 1992 as top seed in the quarter finals against the Indonesian Hermawan Susanto. He punished himself for this by playing mixed doubles in a few tournaments before ending his career at the age of 27.

Olympic gold medal she won in 2004, women's singles World champion in 2003, In 2008, head coach Li Yongbo

Fig. 171: The Chinese players Zhang Ning (left) and Xie Xingfang, finalists in all the big tournaments.

23 Statistics

Olympic Champions

Men's Singles

1972 Rudy Hartono (Indonesia)*
1988 Yang Yang (China)*
1992 Alan Budi Kusuma (Indonesia)
1996 Poul-Erik Høyer-Larsen (Denmark)
2000 Ji Xinpeng (China)
2004 Taufik Hidayat (Indonesia)
2008 Lin Dan (China)

Fig. 173: Zhang Ning

Men's Doubles

1972 Ade Chandra / Christian Hadinata (Indonesia)*
1988 Li Yongbo / Tian Bingyi (China)*
1992 Park Joo-Bong / Kim Moon-Soo (Korea)
1996 Ricky Subagja / Rexy Mainaky (Indonesia)
2000 Tony Gunawan / Candra Wijaya (Indonesia)
2004 Kim Dong-Moon / Ha Tae-Kwon (Korea)
2008 Markis Kido / Hendra Setiawan (Indonesia)

Fig. 174: Markis Kido and Hendra Setiawan

Fig. 172: Taufik Hidayat

Women's Singles

1972 Noriko Nakayama (Japan)*
1988 Han Aiping (China)*
1992 Susi Susanti (Indonesia)
1996 Bang Soo-Hyun (Korea)
2000 Gong Zhichao (China)
2004 Zhang Ning (China)
2008 Zhang Ning (China)

Women's Doubles

1972 not held
1988 Kim Yun-Ja / Chung Soo-Young (Korea)*
1992 Hwang Hye-Young / Chung Soo-Young (Korea)
1996 Ge Fei / Gu Jun (China)
2000 Ge Fei / Gu Jun (China)
2004 Yang Wei / Zhang Jiewen (China)
2008 Du Jing / Yu Yang (China)

*no official Olympic Champion (winner of demonstration event or show competition)

Mixed

1972 Derek Talbot/Gillian Gilks (England)*
1988 Park Joo-Bong/Chung Myung-Hee (Korea)*
1992 not held
1996 Kim Dong-Moon/Gil Young-Ah (Korea)
2000 Zhang Jun/Gao Ling (China)
2004 Zhang Jun/Gao Ling (China)
2008 Lee Yong-Dae/Lee Hyo-Jung (Korea)

World Champions

Men's Singles

1977 Flemming Delfs (Denmark)
1980 Rudy Hartono (Indonesia)
1983 Icuk Sugiarto (Indonesia)
1985 Han Jian (China)
1987 Yang Yang (China)
1989 Yang Yang (China)
1991 Zhao Jianhua (China)
1993 Joko Suprianto (Indonesia)
1995 Heryanto Arbi (Indonesia)
1997 Peter Rasmussen (Denmark)
1999 Sun Jun (China)
2001 Hendrawan (Indonesia)
2003 Xia Xuanze (China)
2005 Taufik Hidayat (Indonesia)
2006 Lin Dan (China)
2007 Lin Dan (China)
2009 Lin Dan (China)

Women's Singles

1977 Lene Køppen (Denmark)
1980 Verawati Wiharjo (Indonesia)
1983 Li Lingwei (China)
1985 Han Aiping (China)
1987 Han Aiping (China)
1989 Li Lingwei (China)

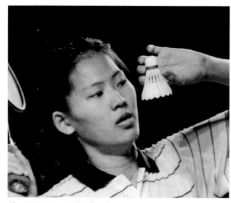

Fig. 175: Verawati Wiharjo

1991 Tang Jiuhong (China)
1993 Susi Susanti (Indonesia)
1995 Ye Zhaoying (China)
1997 Ye Zhaoying (China)
1999 Camilla Martin (Denmark)
2001 Gong Ruina (China)
2003 Zhang Ning (China)
2005 Xie Xingfang (China)
2006 Xie Xingfang (China)
2007 Zhu Lin (China)
2009 Lu Lan (China)

Men's Doubles

1977 Tjun Tjun/Johan Wahjudi (Indonesia)
1980 Christian Hadinata/Ade Chandra (Indonesia)
1983 Steen Fladberg/Jesper Helledie (Denmark)
1985 Park Joo-Bong/Kim Moon-Soo (Korea)
1987 Tian Bingyi/Li Yongbo (China)
1989 Tian Bingyi/Li Jongbo (China)
1991 Park Joo-Bong/Kim Moon-Soo (Korea)
1993 Ricky Subagja/Rudy Gunawan (Indonesia)
1995 Ricky Subagja/Rexy Mainaky (Indonesia)
1997 Candra Wijaya/Sigit Budiarto (Indonesia)
1999 Kim Dong-Moon/Ha Tae-Kwon (Korea)
2001 Halim Haryanto/Tony Gunawan (Indonesia)
2003 Lars Paaske/Jonas Rasmussen (Denmark)
2005 Tony Gunawan/Howard Bach (USA)
2006 Fu Haifeng/Cai Yun (China)
2007 Markis Kido/Hendra Setiawan (Indonesia)
2009 Fu Haifeng/Cai Yun (China)

Women's Doubles

1977 Etsuko Toganoo/Emiko Ueno (Japan)
1980 Nora Perry/Jane Webster (England)
1983 Lin Ying/Wu Dixi (China)
1985 Han Aiping/Li Lingwei (China)
1987 Lin Ying/Guan Weizhen (China)
1989 Lin Ying/Guan Weizhen (China)
1991 Qunhua Nong/Guan Weizhen (China)
1993 Qunhua Nong/Lei Zhou (China)
1995 Gil Young-Ah/Jang Hye-Ock (Korea)
1997 Ge Fei/Gu Jun (China)
1999 Ge Fei/Gu Jun (China)
2001 Huang Sui/Gao Ling (China)
2003 Huang Sui/Gao Ling (China)
2005 Yang Wei/Zhang Jiewen (China)
2006 Huang Sui/Gao Ling (China)
2007 Yang Wei/Zhang Jiewen (China)
2009 Zhang Yawen/Zhao Tingting (China)

Mixed

1977 Steen Skovgaard/Lene Køppen (Denmark)
1980 Christian Hadinata/Imelda Wigoeno (Indonesia)
1983 Thomas Kihlstrøm/Nora Perry (Sweden/England)
1985 Park Joo-Bong/Yoo Sang-Hee (Korea)

1987 Wang Pengren/Shi Fangjing (China)
1989 Park Joo-Bong/Chung Myung-Hee (Korea)
1991 Park Joo-Bong/Chung Myung-Hee (Korea)
1993 Thomas Lund/Catrine Bengtsson (Denmark/Sweden)
1995 Thomas Lund/Marlene Thomsen (Denmark)
1997 Liu Yong/Ge Fei (China)
1999 Kim Dong-Moon/Ra Kyung-Min (Korea)
2001 Zhang Jun/Gao Ling (China)
2003 Kim Dong-Moon/Ra Kyung-Min (Korea)
2005 Nova Widianto/Lilyana Natsir (Indonesia)
2006 Nathan Robertson/Gail Emms (England)
2007 Nova Widianto/Lilyana Natsir (Indonesia)
2009 Thomas Laybourn/Kamilla Rytter Juhl (Denmark)

Fig. 174: Wang Yihan

Fig. 176: Juhl/Layborn

World Junior Champions

Men's Singles

1992 Sun Jun (China)
1994 Chen Gang (China)
1996 Feng Zhu (China)
1998 Zhang Yang (China)
2000 Bao Chunlai (China)
2002 Chen Jin (China)
2004 Chen Jin (China)
2006 Hong Ji-Hoon (Korea)
2007 Chen Long (China)
2008 Wang Zhengming (China)
2009 Houwei Tian (China)

Women's Singles

1992 Kristin Junita (Indonesia)
1994 Wang Chen (China)
1996 Yu Hua (China)
1998 Gong Ruina (China)
2000 Wei Yan (China)
2002 Jiang Yanjiao (China)
2004 Cheng Shao Chieh (Taiwan)
2006 Wang Yihan (China)
2007 Wang Lin (China)
2008 Saina Nehwal (India)
2009 Ratchanok Intanon (Thailand)

Men's Doubles

1992 A. Santoso/Kusno (Indonesia)
1994 Peter Gade Christensen/Peder Nissen (Denmark)
1996 Jeremy Gan Wye Teck/Chan Chong Ming (Malaysia)
1998 Chan Chong Meng/Tao Seng Kok (Malaysia)
2000 Sang Yang/Zheng Bo (China)
2002 Han Sang-Hoon/Park Sung-Hwan (Korea)
2004 Hoon Tien How/Tan Boon Heong (Malaysia)
2006 Lee Yong-Dae/Cho Gun-Woo (Korea)
2007 Chung Eui Seok/Shin Baek Choel (Korea)
2008 Mak Hee Chun/Teo Kok Siang (Malaysia)
2009 Kah Ming Chooi / Yao Han Ow (Malaysia)

Women's Doubles

1992 Gu Jun/Han Jingna (China)
1994 Wang Li/Qian Hong (China)
1996 Gao Ling/Yang Wie (China)
1998 Zhang Jiewen/Xie Xingfang (China)
2000 Zhang Yawen/Wei Yili (China)
2002 Du Jing/Rong Lu (China)
2004 Tian Qing/Yu Yang (China)
2006 Ma Jin/Wang Xiaoli (China)
2007 Xie Jing/Zhong Qianxin (China)
2008 Fu Mingtian/Yao Lei (Singapore)
2009 Jinhua Tang / Huan Xia (China)

Mixed

1992 Jim Laugesen/Rikke Olsen (Denmark)
1994 Zhang Wie/Qian Hong (China)

1996 Wang Wie/Lu Ying (China)
1998 Chan Chong Meng/Joanne Quay (Malaysia)
2000 Sang Yang/Zhang Yawen (China)
2002 Guo Zendong/Yu Yang (China)
2004 He Hanbin/Yu Yang (China)
2006 Lee Yong-Dae/Yoo Hyun-Young (Korea)
2007 Lim Khim Wah/Ng Hui Lin (Malaysia)
2008 Chai Biao/Xie Jung (China)
2009 Maneepong Jongjit / Rodjana Chuthabunditkul (Thailand)

Asian Games
Venue
1951 New Delhi (India)
1954 Manila (Philippines)
1958 Tokyo (Japan)
1962 Jakarta (Indonesia) *
1966 Bangkok (Thailand) *
1970 Bangkok (Thailand) *
1974 Tehran (Iran) *
1978 Bangkok (Thailand) *
1982 New Delhi (India) *
1986 Seoul (Korea) *
1990 Peking (China) *
1994 Hiroshima (Japan) *
1998 Bangkok (Thailand) *
2002 Pusan (Korea) *
2006 Doha (Qatar) *
2010 Guangzhou (China) *

Team Champions
1962 Indonesia (Men); Indonesia (Women)
1966 Indonesia (Men); Japan (Women)
1970 Indonesia (Men); Japan (Women)
1974 China (Men); China (Women)
1978 Indonesia (Men); China (Women)
1982 China (Men); China (Women)
1986 China (Men); China (Women)
1990 China (Men); China (Women)
1994 Indonesia (Men), Korea (Women)
1998 Indonesia (Men), China (Women)
2002 Korea (Men); China (Women)
2006 China (Men), China (Women)

Men's Singles
1962 Tan Joe Hok (Indonesia)
1966 Muldjadi (Indonesia)
1970 Punch Gunalan (Malaysia)
1974 Hou Chia Chang
1978 Liem Siwe King (Indonesia)
1982 Han Jian (China)
1986 Zhao Jianhua (China)

* Badminton in the program

1990 Zhao Jianhua (China)
1994 Heryanto Arbi (Indonesia)
1998 Dong Jiong (China)
2002 Taufik Hidayat (Indonesia)
2006 Taufik Hidayat (Indonesia)

Fig. 178: Zhou Mi

Women's Singles
1962 Minarni (Indonesia)
1966 Norioko Takagi (Japan)
1970 Hiroe Yuki (Japan)
1974 Chen Yu Niang
1978 Liang Chiu Sia (China)
1982 Zhang Ailing (China)
1986 Han Aiping (China)
1990 Tang Jiuhong (China)
1994 Bang Soo-Hyun (Korea)
1998 Kanako Yonekura (Japan)
2002 Zhou Mi (China)
2006 Wang Chen (Hong Kong)

Men's Doubles
1962 Tan Yee Khan/Ng Boon Bee (Malaysia)
1966 Tan Yee Khan/Ng Boon Bee (Malaysia)
1970 Punch Gunalan/Ng Boon Bee (Malaysia)
1974 Tjun Tjun/Johann Wahjudi (Indonesia)
1978 Christian Hadinata/Ade Chandra (Indonesia)
1982 Icuk Sugiarto/Christian Hadinata (Indonesia)
1986 Park Joo-Bong/Kim Moon-Soo (Korea)
1990 Li Yongbo/Tian Bingyi (China)
1994 Ricky Subagja/Rexy Mainaky (Indonesia)
1998 Ricky Subagja/Rexy Mainaky (Indonesia)
2002 Lee Dong-Soo/Yoo Yung-Sung (Korea)
2006 Koo Kien Keat/Tian Boon Heong (Malaysia)

Women's Doubles

1962 Minarni / Retno Koestijah (Indonesia)
1966 Minarni / Retno Koestijah (Indonesia)
1970 Machiko Aizawa / Etsuko Takenaka (Japan)
1974 Liang Chiu-Hsia / Chen Hui Ming (China)
1978 Verwaty / Imelga (Indonesia)
1982 Sun Ai Hwang / Heung Seuk Kang (Korea)
1986 Lin Ying / Guan Weizhen (China)
1990 Guan Weizhen / Nong Qunhua (China)
1994 Shim Eun-Jung / Jang Hye-Ock (Korea)
1998 Ge Fei / Gu Jun (China)
2002 Ra Kyung-Min / Lee Kyung-Won (Korea)
2006 Gao Ling / Huang Sui (China)

Mixed

1962 not held
1966 Teh Kew San / Rosalind Singha Ang (Malaysia)
1970 Ng Boon Bee / Sylvia Ng (Malaysia)
1974 Christain Hadinata / R. Masli (Indonesia)
1978 Tan Hsien Hu / Hang Ai Ling (China)
1982 Christain Hadinata / Ivana Lie (Indonesia)
1986 Park Joo-Bong / Chung Myung-Hee (Korea)
1990 Park Joo-Bong / Chung Myung-Hee (Korea)
1994 Yoo Yong-Sung / Chung So-Young (Korea)
1998 Kim Dong-Moon / Ra Kyung-Min (Korea)
2002 Kim Dong-Moon / Ra Kyung-Min (Korea)
2006 Zheng Bo / Gao Ling (China)

Asian Championchips

Men's Singles

1962 Teh Kew San (Malaysia)
1965 Dinesh Khanna (India)
1969 Muljadi (Indien)
1971 Tan Aik Mong (Malaysia)
1976 Hou Chia Chang (China)
1983 Chen Changjie (China)
1985 Zhao Jianhua (China)
1987 Misbun Sidek (Malaysia)
1988 Yang Yang (China)
1991 Rashid Sidek (Malaysia)
1992 Rashid Sidek (Malaysia)
1994 Foo Kok Keong (Korea)
1995 Park Sung-Woo (Korea)
1996 Jeffer Rosobin (Indonesia)
1997 Sun Jun (China)
1998 Chen Gang (China)
1999 Chen Hong (China)
2000 Taufik Hidayat (Indonesia)
2001 Xia Xuanze (China)
2002 Sony Dwi Kuncoro (Indonesia)
2003 Sony Dwi Kuncoro (Indonesia)
2004 Taufik Hidayat (Indonesia)
2005 Sony Dwi Kuncoro (Indonesia)
2006 Lee Chong Wei (Malaysia)

Fig. 179: Sony Dwi Kuncoro

2007 Taufik Hidayat (Indonesia)
2008 Park Sung-Hwan (Korea)
2009 Bao Chunlai (China)

Women's Singles

1962 Minarni (Indonesia)
1965 Angela Bairstow (England)
1969 Pang Yuet Mui (Hong Kong)
1971 Utami Dewi (Indonesia)
1976 Liang Chiu Hsia China)
1983 Sang Hee-Yoo (Korea)
1985 Zheng Yuli (China)
1987 Elizabeth Latief (Indonesia)
1988 Li Lingwei (China)
1991 Yuliani Santoso (Indonesia)
1992 Ye Zahoying (China)
1994 Ye Zhaoying (China)
1995 Ye Zhaoying (China)
1996 Gong Zhichao (China)
1997 Yao Yan (China)
1998 Ye Zhaoying (China)
1999 Ye Zhaoying (China)
2000 Xie Xingfang (China)
2001 Zhang Ning (China)
2002 Zhou Mi (China)
2003 Wang Chen (Hong Kong)
2004 Jun Yae-Youn (Korea)
2005 Wang Chen (Hong Kong)
2006 Wang Chen (Hong Kong)
2007 Jiang Yanjiao (China)
2008 Jiang Yanjiao (China)
2009 Zhu Lin (China)

Men's Doubles

1962 Ng Boon Bee/Tan Yee Khan (Malaysia)
1965 Narong Pomchim/Chavelert Chumkam (Thailand)
1969 Ng Boon Bee/Punch Gunalan (Malaysia)
1971 Indra Gunawan/Nara Sudjana (Indonesia)
1976 Tjun Tjun/Ade Chandra (Indonesia)
1983 Jiang Guoliang/He Shangquan (China)
1985 Park Joo-Bong/Kim Moon-Soo (Korea)
1987 Liem Swie King/Bobby Ertanto (Indonesia)
1988 Shinji Matsuura/Shuji Matsuno (Japan)
1991 Park Joo-Bong/Kim Moon-Soo (Korea)
1992 Razif Sidek/Jalani Sidek (Malaysia)
1994 Chen Kang/Chen Hongyong (China)
1995 Cheah Soon Kit/Yap Kim Hock (Malaysia)
1996 Ade Sutrisna/Candra Wijaya (Indonesia)
1997 Denny Kantono/Antonius (Indonesia)
1998 Kang Kyung-Jin/Ha Tae-Kwon (Korea)
1999 Ha Tae-Kwon/Kim Dong-Moon (Korea)
2000 Rexy Mainaky/Tony Gunawan (Indonesia)
2001 Trikus Haryanto/Bambang Suprianto (Indonesia)
2002 Ha Tae-Kwon/Kim Dong-Moon (Korea)
2003 Lee Dong-Soo/Yoo Yong-Sung (Korea)
2004 Trikus Haryanto/Budiarto Sigit (Indonesia)
2005 Markis Kido/Hendra Setiawan (Indonesia)
2006 Choong Tan Fock/Lee Wan Wah (Malaysia)
2007 Choong Tan Fock/Lee Wan Wah (Malaysia)
2008 Lee Young-Dae/Jung Jae-Sung (Korea)
2009 Hendra Setiawan/Markis Kido (Indonesia)

Women's Doubles

1962 Jap Happy/Corry Kawilarang (Indonesia)
1965 Ursula Smith/Angela Bairstow (England)
1969 Lee Young-Soon/Kang Young-Sin (Korea)
1971 Retno Kustija/Intan (Indonesia)
1976 Theresia Widiastuti/Regina Masli (Indonesia)
1983 Guan Weizen/Fan Ming (China)
1985 Kim Yun-Ja/Yoo Sang-Hee (Korea)
1987 Hwang Hye-Young/Chung Myung-Hee (Korea)
1988 Shi W./Zhou Lei (China)
1991 Hwang Hye-Young/Chung So-Young (Korea)
1992 Wu Yuhong/Pan Li (China)
1994 Ge Fei/Gu Jun (China)
1995 Ge Fei/Gu Jun (China)
1996 Eliza/Finarsih (Indonesia)
1997 Liu Zhong/Huang Nanyan (China)
1998 Ge Fei/Gu Jun (China)
1999 Ge Fei/Gu Jun (China)
2000 Lee Hyo-Jung/Yim Kyung-Jin (Korea)
2001 Gao Ling/Huang Sui (China)
2002 Zhang Jiewen/Yang Wei (China)
2003 Ra Kyung-Min/Lee Kyung-Won (Korea)
2004 Lee Hyo-Jung/Lee Kyung-Won (Korea)
2005 Lee Hyo-Jung/Lee Kyung-Won (Korea)

2006 Yu Yang/Du Jing (Korea)
2007 Yang Wei/Zhao Tingting (China)
2008 Yang Wei/Zhang Jiewen (China)
2009 Ma Jin/Wang Xiaoli (China)

Mixed

1962 Lim Say Hup/Ng Mei Ling (Malyasia)
1965 Tan Yee Khan/Angela Bairstow (Malaysia/England)
1969 not held
1971 Christian Hadinata/Retno Kustijah (Indonesia)
1976 not held
1983 Park Joo-Bong/Kim Yun-Ja (Korea)
1985 not held
1987 not held
1988 not held
1991 Park Joo-Bong/Chung Myeong-Hee (Korea)
1992 Joko Mardiano/Sri Untari (Indonesia)
1994 Chen Xingdong/Sun Man (China)
1995 Liu Yong/Ge Fei (China)
1996 Trikus Haryanto/Lili Tampi (Indonesia)
1997 Zhang Jun/Liu Lu (China)
1998 Kim Dong-Moon/Ra Kyung-Min (Korea)
1999 Kim Dong-Moon/Ra Kyung-Min (Korea)
2000 Bambang Suprianto/Minarti Timur (Indonesia)
2001 Kim Dong-Moon/Ra Kyung-Min (Korea)
2002 Zhang Jun/Gao Ling (China)
2003 Nova Widianto/Vita Marissa (Indonesia)
2004 Kim Dong-Moon/Ra Kyung-Min (Korea)
2005 Sudket Prapakamol/Saralee Thoungthongkam (Thailand)
2006 Nova Widianto/Lilyana Natsir (Indonesia)
2007 He Hanbin/Yu Yang (China)
2008 Flandy Limpele/Vita Marissa (Indonesia)
2009 Lee Young-Dae/Lee Hyo-Jung (Korea)

Commonwealth Games
Venue

1930 Hamilton (Canada)
1934 London (England)
1938 Sydney (Australia)
1950 Auckland (New Zealand)
1954 Vancouver (Canada)
1958 Cardiff (Wales)
1962 Perth (Australia)
1966 Kingston (Jamaica) *
1970 Edinburgh (Scotland) *
1974 Christchurch (New Zealand) *
1978 Edmonton (Canada) *
1982 Brisbane (Australia) *
1986 Edinburgh (Scotland) *
1990 Auckland (New Zealand) *
1994 Victoria (Canada) *
1998 Kuala Lumpur (Malaysia) *

*Badminton in the program

2002 Manchester (England) *
2006 Melbourne (Australia) *
2010 New Delhi (India) *

Team Champions

1966 not held
1970 not held
1974 not held
1978 England
1982 England
1986 England
1990 England
1994 England
1998 Malaysia (men); England (women)
2002 England
2006 Malaysia

Fig. 180: Lee Chong Wei

Men's Singles

1966 Tan Aik Huang (Malaysia)
1970 Jamie Paulson (Canada)
1974 Punch Gunalan (Malaysia)
1978 Prakash Padukone (India)
1982 Syed Modi (India)
1986 Steve Baddeley (England)
1990 Rashid Sidek (Malaysia)
1994 Rashid Sidek (Malaysia)
1998 Wong Choong Hann (Malaysia)
2002 Muhammad Hafiz Hashim (Malaysia)
2006 Lee Chong Wei (Malaysia)

Women's Singles

1966 Angela Bairston (England)
1970 Margaret Beck (England)

1974 Gillian Gilks (England)
1978 Sylvia Ng (Malaysia)
1982 Helen Troke (England)
1986 Helen Troke (England)
1990 Fiona Smith (England)
1994 Lisa Campbell (Australia)
1998 Kelly Morgan (Wales)
2002 Li Li (Singapore)
2006 Tracey Hallam (England)

Men's Doubles

1966 Tan Aik Huang / Yew Cheng Hoe (Malaysia)
1970 Ng Boon Bee / Punch Gunalan (Malaysia)
1974 Derek Talbot / Elliot Stuart (England)
1978 Ray Stevens / Michael Tredgett (England)
1982 Razif Sidek / Beng Teong Ong (Malaysia)
1986 Billy Gilliland / Dan Travers (Scotland)
1990 Razif Sidek / Jalani Sidek (Malaysia)
1994 Cheah Soon-Kit / Soo Beng Kiang (Malaysia)
1998 Chong Tan Fooh / Lee Wan Wah (Malaysia)
2002 Chew Chong Eng / Chan Chong Ming (Malaysia)
2006 Chan Chong Ming / Koo Kien Keat (Malaysia)

Women's Doubles

1966 Helen Horton / Ursula Smith (England)
1970 Margaret Boxall / Susan Whetnall (England)
1974 Margaret Beck / Gillian Gilks (England)
1978 Nora Perry / Anne Statt (England)
1982 Claire Backhouse / Johanne Falardean (Canada)
1986 Gillian Clark / Gillian Gowers (England)
1990 Fiona Smith / Sara Sankey (England)
1994 Joanne Wright / Jo Muggeridge (England)
1998 Donna Kellogg / Joanne Goode (England)
2002 Ang Li Peng / Lim Pek Siah (Malaysia)
2006 Wong Pei Tty / Chin Eei Hui (Malaysia)

Mixed

1966 Roger Mills / Angela Bairstow (England)
1970 Derek Talbot / Margaret Boxall (England)
1974 Derek Talbot Talbot / Gillian Gilks (England)
1978 Michael Tredgett / Nora Perry (England)
1982 Martin Dew / Karen Chapman (England)
1986 Mike Scandolera / Audrey Tuckey (Australia)
1990 Chan Chi Choi / Amy Chan (Hong Kong)
1994 Chris Hunt / Gillian Clark (England)
1998 Simon Archer / Joanne Goode (England)
2002 Simon Archer / Joanne Goode (England)
2006 Nathan Robertson / Gail Emms (England)

All England Open (since 1899)
Men's Singles

1983 Luan Jin (China)
1984 Morten Frost (Denmark)
1985 Zhao Jianhua (China)

1986 Morten Frost (Denmark)
1987 Morten Frost (Denmark)
1988 Ib Frederiksen (Denmark)
1989 Yang Yang (China)
1990 Zhao Jianhua (China)
1991 Ardy Wiranata (Indonesia)
1992 Liu Jun (China)
1993 Heryanto Arbi (Indonesia)
1994 Heryanto Arbi (Indonesia)
1995 Poul-Erik Høyer-Larsen (Denmark)
1996 Poul-Erik Høyer-Larsen (Denmark)
1997 Dong Jiong (China)
1998 Sun Jun (China)
1999 Peter Gade Christensen (Denmark)
2000 Xia Xuanze (China)
2001 Pullela Gopichand (India)
2002 Chen Hong (China)
2003 Muhammad Hafiz Hashim (Malaysia)
2004 Lin Dan (China)
2005 Chen Hong (China)
2006 Lin Dan (China)
2007 Lin Dan (China)
2008 Chen Jin (China)
2009 Lin Dan (China)

Fig. 181: Lin Dan

Women's Singles

1983 Zhang Ailing (China)
1984 Li Lingwei (China)
1985 Han Aiping (China)
1986 Kim Jun-Ja (Korea)
1987 Kirsten Larsen (Denmark)
1988 Gu Jiaminng (China)
1989 Li Lingwei (China)

Fig. 182: Tine Rasmussen

1990 Susi Susanti (Indonesia)
1991 Susi Susanti (Indonesia)
1992 Tang Jiuhong (China)
1993 Susi Susanti (Indonesia)
1994 Susi Susanti (Indonesia)
1995 Lim Xiao Qing (Sweden)
1996 Bang Soo-Hyun (Korea)
1997 Ye Zhaoying (China)
1998 Ye Zhaoying (China)
1999 Ye Zhaoying (China)
2000 Gong Zhichao (China)
2001 Gong Zhichao (China)
2002 Camilla Martin (Denmark)
2003 Zhou Mi (China)
2004 Gong Ruina (China)
2005 Xie Xingfang (China)
2006 Xie Xingfang (China)
2007 Xie Xingfang (China)
2008 Tine Rasmussen (Denmark)
2009 Wang Yihan (China)

Men's Doubles

1983 Thomas Kihlstrom / Stefan Karlsson (Sweden)
1984 Rudy Heryanto / Hariatmanto Kartono (Indonesia)
1985 Kim Moon-Soo / Park Joo-Bong (Korea)
1986 Kim Moon-Soo / Park Joo-Bong (Korea)
1987 Li Yongbo / Tian Bingyi (China)
1988 Li Yongbo / Tian Bingyi (China)
1989 Lee Sang-Bok / Park Joo-Bong (Korea)
1990 Kim Moon-Soo / Park Joo-Bong (Korea)
1991 Li Yongbo / Tian Bingyi (China)
1992 Rudy Gunawan / Eddy Hartono (Indonesia)
1993 Thomas Lund / Jon Holst-Christensen (Denmark)
1994 Bambang Suprianto / Rudy Gunawan (Indonesia)

Fig. 183: Fu Haifeng/Cai Yun

1995 Rexy Mainaky/Ricky Subagja (Indonesia)
1996 Rexy Mainaky/Ricky Subagja (Indonesia)
1997 Kang Kyung-Jin/Ha Tae-Kwon (Korea)
1998 Lee Dong-Soo/Yoo Yong-Sung (Korea)
1999 Tony Gunawan/Candra Wijaya (Indonesia)
2000 Ha Tae-Kwon/Kim Dong-Moon (Korea)
2001 Tony Gunawan/Halim Haryanto (Indonesia)
2002 Ha Tae-Kwon/Kim Dong-Moon (Korea)
2003 Sigit Budiarto/Candra Wijaya (Indonesia)
2004 Jens Eriksen/Martin Lundgaard Hansen (Denmark)
2005 Fu Haifeng/Cai Yun (China)
2006 Jens Eriksen/Martin Lundgaard Hansen (Denmark)
2007 Koo Kien Keat/Tan Boon Heong (Malaysia)
2008 Jung Ja-Sung/Lee Yoong-Dae (Korea)
2009 Fu Haifeng/Cai Yun (China)

Women's Doubles

1983 Xu Rong/Wu Jianqiu (China)
1984 Lin Ying/Wu Dixi (China)
1985 Han Aiping/Li Lingwei (China)
1986 Chung Myung-Hee/Hwang Hye-Young (Korea)
1987 Chung Myung-Hee/Hwang Hye-Young (Korea)
1988 Chung So-Young/Kim Jun-Ja (Korea)
1989 Chung Myung-Hee/Chung So-Young (Korea)
1990 Chung Myung-Hee/Hwang Hye-Young (Korea)
1991 Chung So-Young/Hwang Hye-Young (Korea)
1992 Lin Yanfen/Yao Fen (China)
1993 Chung So-Young/Gil Young-Ah (Korea)
1994 Chung So-Young/Gil Young-Ah (Korea)
1995 Kim Mee-Hyang/Kim Shin-Yong (Korea)
1996 Ge Fei/Gu Jun (China)
1997 Ge Fei/Gu Jun (China)
1998 Ge Fei/Gu Jun (China)
1999 Chung Jae-Hee/Ra Kyung-Min (Korea)
2000 Ge Fei/Gu Jun (China)
2001 Gao Ling/Huang Sui (China)
2002 Gao Ling/Huang Sui (China)
2003 Gao Ling/Huang Sui (China)

2004 Gao Ling/Huang Sui (China)
2005 Gao Ling/Huang Sui (China)
2006 Gao Ling/Huang Sui (China)
2007 Wei Yili/Zhang Yawen (China)
2008 Lee Kyung-Won/Lee Hyo-Jung (Korea)
2009 Zhang Yawen/Zhao Tingting (China)

Mixed

1983 Thomas Kihlstrom/Nora Perry (Sweden/England)
1984 Martin Dew/Gillian Gilks (England)
1985 Billy Gilliland/Nora Perry (Scotland/England)
1986 Park Joo-Bong/Chung Myung-Hee (Korea)
1987 Lee Deuk-Choon/Chung Myung-Hee (Korea)
1988 Wang Pengren/Shi Fangjing (China)
1989 Park Joo-Bong/Chung Myung-Hee (Korea)
1990 Park Joo-Bong/Chung Myung-Hee (Korea)
1991 Park Joo-Bong/Chung Myung-Hee (Korea)
1992 Thomas Lund/Pernille Dupont (Denmark)
1993 Jon Holst-Christensen/Grete Mogensen (Denmark)
1994 Nick Pointing/Joanne Wright (Engand)
1995 Thomas Lund/Marlene Thomsen (Denmark)
1996 Park Joo-Bong/Ra Kyung-Min (Korea)
1997 Liu Yong/Ge Fei (China)
1998 Kim Dong-Moon/Ra Kyung-Min (Korea)
1999 Simon Archer/Joanne Goode (England)
2000 Kim Dong-Moon/Ra Kyung-Min (Korea)
2001 Zhang Jun/Gao Ling (China)
2002 Kim Dong-Moon/Ra Kyung-Min (Korea)
2003 Zhang Jun/Gao Ling (China)
2004 Kim Dong-Moon/Ra Kyung-Min (Korea)
2005 Nathan Robertson/Gail Emms (England)
2006 Zhang Jun/Gao Ling (China)
2007 Zheng Bo/Gao Ling (China)
2008 Zheng Bo/Gao Ling (China)
2009 He Hanbin/Yu Yang (China)

Fig. 184: Nathan Robertson/Gail Emms

European Championship

Men's Singles

1968 Sture Johnsson (Sweden)
1970 Sture Johnsson (Sweden)
1972 Wolfgang Bochow (Germany)
1974 Sture Johnsson (Sweden)
1976 Flemming Delfs (Denmark)
1978 Flemming Delfs (Denmark)
1980 Flemming Delfs (Denmark)
1982 Jens-Peter Nierhoff (Denmark)
1984 Morten Frost (Denmark)
1986 Morten Frost (Denmark)
1988 Darren Hall (England)
1990 Steve Baddeley (England)
1992 Poul-Erik Høyer-Larsen (Denmark)
1994 Poul-Erik Høyer-Larsen (Denmark)
1996 Poul-Erik Høyer-Larsen (Denmark)
1998 Peter Gade Christensen (Denmark)
2000 Peter Gade Christensen (Denmark)
2002 Peter Rasmussen (Denmark)
2004 Peter Gade Christensen (Denmark)
2006 Peter Gade Christensen (Denmark)
2008 Kenneth Jonassen (Denmark)

Fig 185: Kenneth Jonassen

Women's Singles

1968 Irmgard Latz (Germany)
1970 Eva Twedberg (Sweden)
1972 Margaret Beck (England)
1974 Gillian Gilks (England)
1976 Gillian Gilks (England)
1978 Lene Køppen (Denmark)
1980 Liselotte Blumer (Switzerland)
1982 Lene Køppen (Denmark)
1984 Helen Troke (England)
1986 Helen Troke (England)
1988 Kirsten Larsen (Denmark)
1990 Pernille Nedergaard (Denmark)
1992 Pernille Nedergaard (Denmark)
1994 Lim Xiao Qing (Sweden)
1996 Camilla Martin (Denmark)
1998 Camilla Martin (Denmark)
2000 Camilla Martin (Denmark)
2002 Yao Jie (Netherlands)
2004 Mia Audina (Netherlands)
2006 Xu Huaiwen (Germany)
2008 Xu Huaiwen (Germany)

Fig. 186: Xu Huaiwen

Men's Doubles

1968 David Eddy/Roger Powell (England)
1970 Elo Hansen/Per Walsöe (Denmark)
1972 Willy Braun/Roland Maywald (Germany)
1974 Willy Braun/Roland Maywald (Germany)
1976 Ray Stevens/Mike Tredgett (England)
1978 Ray Stevens/Mike Tredgett (England)
1980 Claes Nordin/Stefan Karlsson (Sweden)
1982 Thomas Kihlström/Stefan Karlsson (Sweden)
1984 Mike Tredgett/Matin Dew (England)
1986 Steen Fladberg/Jesper Helledie (Denmark)
1988 Jens-Peter Nierhoff/Michael Kjeldsen (Denmark)
1990 Henrik Svarrer/Jan Paulsen (Denmark)
1992 Thomas Lund/Jon Holst-Christensen (Denmark)
1994 Chris Hunt/Simon Archer (England)
1996 Thomas Lund/Jon Holst-Christensen (Denmark)
1998 Chris Hunt/Simon Archer (England)
2000 Jens Eriksen/Jesper Larsen (Denmark)
2002 Jens Eriksen/Martin Lundgaard Hansen (Denmark)
2004 Jens Eriksen/Martin Lundgaard Hansen (Denmark)
2006 Jens Eriksen/Martin Lundgaard Hansen (Denmark)
2008 Jonas Rasmussen/Lars Paaske (Denmark)

Women's Doubles

1968 Margaret Boxall / Susan Whetnal (England)
1970 Margaret Boxall / Susan Whetnal (England)
1972 Gillian Gilks / Judy Hashman (England)
1974 Gillian Gilks / Margaret Beck (England)
1976 Gillian Gilks / Susan Whetnal (England)
1978 Nora Perry / Anne Statt (England)
1980 Jane Webster / Nora Perry (England)
1982 Gillian Gilks / Gillian Clark (England)
1984 Karen Chapman / Gillian Clark (England)
1986 Gillian Clark / Gillian Gowers (England)
1988 Dorte Kjaer / Nettie Nielsen (Denmark)
1990 Dorte Kjaer / Nettie Nielsen (Denmark)
1992 Christine Magnusson / Lim Xiao Qing (Sweden)
1994 Christine Magnusson / Lim Xiao Qing (Sweden)
1996 Rikke Olsen / Helene Kirkegaard (Denmark)
1998 Rikke Olsen / Marlene Thomsen (Denmark)
2000 Donna Kellogg / Joanne Goode (England)
2002 Jane Bramsen / Ann-Lou Jörgensen (Denmark)
2004 Mia Audina / Lotte Bruil (Netherlands)
2006 Donna Kellogg / Gail Emms (England)
2008 Kamilla Rytter Juhl / Lena Frier Kristiansen (Denmark)

Fig. 187: Jens Eriksen / Martin Lundgaard Hansen

Mixed

1968 Tony Jordan / Susan Whetnall (England)
1970 David Eddy / Susan Whetnall (England)
1972 Derek Talbot / Gillian Gilks (England)
1974 Derek Talbot / Gillian Gilks (England)
1976 Derek Talbot / Gillian Gilks (England)
1978 Mike Tredgett / Nora Perry (England)
1980 Mike Tredgett / Nora Perry (England)
1982 Martin Dew / Gillian Gilks (England)
1984 Martin Dew / Gillian Gilks (England)
1986 Martin Dew / Gillian Gilks (England)
1988 Steen Fladberg / Gillian Clark (England)
1990 Jon Holst-Christensen / Grete Mogensen (Denmark)
1992 Thomas Lund / Pernille Dupont (Denmark)

1994 Michael Søgaard / Catrine Bengtsson (Denmark / Sweden)
1996 Michael Søgaard / Rikke Olsen (Denmark)
1998 Michael Søgaard / Rikke Olsen (Denmark)
2000 Michael Søgaard / Rikke Olsen (Denmark)
2002 Jens Eriksen / Mette Scholdager (Denmark)
2004 Nathan Robertson / Gail Emms (England)
2006 Thomas Laybourn / Kamilla Juhl (Denmark)
2008 Anthony Clark / Donna Kellogg (England)

Thomas Cup
(Men's team World Championships)

Venue (Final)

1949 Preston (England)
1952 Singapore (Singapore)
1955 Singapore (Singapore)
1958 Singapore (Singapore)
1961 Jakarta (Indonesia)
1964 Tokyo (Japan)
1967 Jakarta (Indonesia)
1970 Kuala Lumpur (Malaysia)
1973 Jakarta (Indonesia)
1976 Bangkok (Thailand)
1979 Jakarta (Indonesia)
1982 London (England)
1984 Kuala Lumpur (Malaysia)
1986 Jakarta (Indonesia)
1988 Kuala Lumpur (Malaysia)
1990 Nagoya (Japan)
1992 Kuala Lumpur (Malaysia)
1994 Jakarta (Indonesia)
1996 Hong Kong (Hong Kong)
1998 Hong Kong (Hong Kong)
2000 Kuala Lumpur (Malaysia)
2002 Guangzhou (China)
2004 Jakarta (Indonesia)
2006 Tokyo + Sendai (Japan)
2008 Jakarta (Indonesia)
2010 Kuala Lumpur (Malaysia)

Winners

1949 Malaya (10*)
1952 Malaya (12)
1955 Malaya (21)
1958 Indonesia (19)
1961 Indonesia (19)
1964 Indonesia (26)
1967 Malaysia (23)
1970 Indonesia (25)
1973 Indonesia (23)
1976 Indonesia (26)
1979 Indonesia (21)
1982 China (26)
1984 Indonesia (34)

* total number of participating countries

1986 China (38)
1988 China (35)
1990 China (53)
1992 Malaysia (54)
1994 Indonesia (51)
1996 Indonesia (56)
1998 Indonesia (49)
2000 Indonesia (48)
2002 Indonesia (50)
2004 China (61)
2006 China (70)
2008 China (59)

Fig. 188: Sudirman Cup: The chinese team celebrates the win in 2005

Uber Cup

(Women's team World Championships)

Venue (Final**)

1957 Lytham St Anne's (England)
1960 Philadelphia (USA)
1963 Wilmington (USA)
1966 Wellington (New Zealand)
1969 Tokyo (Japan)
1972 Tokyo (Japan)
1975 Jakarta (Indonesia)
1978 Auckland (New Zealand)
1981 Tokyo (Japan)

Winners

1957 USA (11*)
1960 USA (14)
1963 USA (11)
1966 Japan (17)
1969 Japan (19)
1972 Japan (17)
1975 Indonesia (14)
1978 Japan (16)
1981 Japan (15)
1984 China (23)
1986 China (34)
1988 China (31)
1990 China (42)
1992 China (44)
1994 Indonesia (44)
1996 Indonesia (47)
1998 China (40)
2000 China (43)
2002 China (44)
2004 China (50)
2006 China (56)
2008 China (50)

Sudirman Cup

Venue

1989 Jakarta (Indonesia)
1991 Copenhagen (Denmark)
1993 Birmingham (England)
1995 Lausanne (Switzerland)
1997 Glasgow (Scotland)
1999 Copenhagen (Denmark)
2001 Seville (Spain)
2003 s'Hertogenbosch (Netherlands)
2005 Peking (China)
2007 Glasgow (Scotland)
2009 Guangzhou (China)

Team Champions

1989 Indonesia (28*)
1991 Korea (35)
1993 Korea (40)
1995 China (49)
1997 China (59)
1999 China (50)
2001 China (53)
2003 Korea (50)
2005 China (41)
2007 China (48)
2009 China (34)

Hall of Fame

Inaugural Members

S S C Dolby
Sir George Thomas
Betty Uber
Herbert Scheele

* total number of participating countries

** Since 1984, the Uber Cup has been held in conjunction with the Thomas Cup, so please see Thomas Cup for venue.

1997

Tonny Ahm (Denmark)
Frank Devlin (Ireland)
David Freeman (USA)
Rudy Hartono (Indonesia)
Erland Kops (Denmark)
Major John McCallum (Ireland)
Stellan Mohlin (Sweden)
Ralph Nichols (England)
Craig Reedie (Scotland)
Eddy Choong (Malaysia)
Judy Hashman (Devlin) (USA/England)
Dick Sudirman (Indonesia)
Finn Kobbero (Denmark)

1998

David Choong (Malaysia)
Han Aiping (China)
Jorgen Hammergaard Hansen (Denmark)
Morten Frost Hansen (Denmark)
Lene Køppen (Denmark)
Li Lingwei (China)
Meriel Lucas (England)
Ng Boon Bee (Malaysia)
Ong Poh Lim (Malaysia)
Tan Yee Khan (Malaysia)

1999

Gillian Gilks (England)
Nora Perry (England)
Ulla Strand (Denmark)
Margaret Tragett (England)
Margaret Varner Bloss (USA)
Wong Peng Soon (Singapore)

2000

Kirsten Thorndahl (Denmark)
Charoen Wattanasin (Thailand)

2001

Christian Hadinata (Indonesia)
Park Joo Bong (Korea)

2002

Chen Yuniang (China)
Hou Jiachang (China)
Kim Moon Soo (Korea)
Liem Swie King (Indonesia)
Tang Xianhu (China)
Hiroe Yuki (Japan)

2003

Chung Myeong Hee (Korea)
Chung So Young (Korea)

2004

Susi Susanti (Indonesia)

2009

Ethel Thompson (England)
Lu Shengrong (China)
Thomas Lund (Denmark)
Ge Fei (China)
Gu Jun (China)

More statistics on: www.bernd-volker-brahms.de

Useful Addresses:

USA Badminton
One Olympic Plaza
Colorado Springs, CO 80909
phone: (719) 866-4808
fax: (719)886-4507
            usab@usabadminton.org
            www.usabadminton.org

Badminton England,
National Badminton Centre
Milton Keynes,
MK8 9LA
phone: 01908/268400
            www.badmintonengland.co.uk

Photo Credits:

Bernd-Volker Brahms (all, unless otherwise indicated), Mark Speight (page 3 right, 53, 55, 66, 92), Archive of the Badminton Association of Germany (page 143, 145 (right), 157 (right)), Louis Ross (page 150 (left), 151 (right), 157 (left)), Victor Sport (page 7, 8, 11, 12, 15 (bottom), 17, 133 (bottom)); Nike (page 19), Melanie Reinsch (all graphics), Ubbo Busboom (Cartoon, page 175)

Cover design: Sabine Groten

Cover photos: Imago Sportfotodienst GmbH; ©Yang MingQi/Fotolia.com

Fig. 189: Hans-Jörg Brahms and Maria Neiling

Special thanks to:

Kerstin Singer, Horst Rosenstock, Hans-Jörg Brahms, Maria Neiling, Ubbo Busboom, Melanie Reinsch, Manfred Kehrberg, Claudia Pauli, Martin Kranitz, Victor Sport.